All the Cozy
CHRISTMAS FEELS

THESE ARE A FEW OF OUR FAVORITE THINGS

LAURA J. WALKER

WHITAKER HOUSE

Unless otherwise noted, all Scripture quotations are taken from the *Holy Bible, New International Version*®, NIV® Copyright © 1973, 1978, 1984, 2011 by Biblica, Inc.® Used by permission. All rights reserved worldwide. The "NIV" and "New International Version" are trademarks registered in the United States Patent and Trademark Office by Biblica, Inc.® Scripture quotations marked (mev) are taken from the Modern English Version. Copyright © 2014 by Military Bible Association. Used by permission. All rights reserved.

All the Cozy Christmas Feels
These Are a Few of Our Favorite Things

Laura J. Walker

ISBN: 979-8-88769-445-0
eBook ISBN: 979-8-88769-446-7
Printed in the United States of America
© 2025 by Laura J. Walker

Whitaker House
1030 Hunt Valley Circle
New Kensington, PA 15068
www.whitakerhouse.com

Library of Congress Control Number: 2025903920

No part of this book may be reproduced or transmitted in any form or by any means, electronic or mechanical—including photocopying, recording, or by any information storage and retrieval system—without permission in writing from the publisher. Please direct your inquiries to permissionseditor@whitakerhouse.com.

1 2 3 4 5 6 7 8 9 10 11 ⨃ 32 31 30 29 28 27 26 25

For Michael, aka my Renaissance man and "Mr. Christmas," with all my love

Contents

Foreword by Davis Bunn 7

Introduction 11

   1. Merry Yuletide Journey 15

   2. O Come, All Ye Fruitcakes 21

   3. Deck the Halls 35

   4. Of Craft Fairs and Homemade Gifts 41

   5. Those Not-so-Silent Nights 51

   6. Here Comes Doggy Paws, Here Comes Kitty Claws ... 57

   7. Making New Traditions, Breaking Old Traditions 65

   8. Christmas Without Children 75

   9. Taking the Bah Out of Humbug 85

  10. You'll Go Down in His Story 89

  11. That's the Woman Who Rocks 99

12. Rent-a-Kid and Other Ways to Make
    the Yuletide Bright 107
13. What Happens When You *Can't* Go Home
    for Christmas? 113
14. Less Isn't Always More (Deck the Halls, Part Two) ... 121
15. Sing Out! A Totally Subjective List of Favorite
    Christmas Music 131
16. Attaboy, Clarence! A Definitive Holiday
    Movie Guide 137

About the Author 160

Foreword

When I was twenty years old, I accepted an invitation to do a master of science in international finance and economics in London. My plan was to complete the studies then return to North Carolina, do my law degree, and join the firm my grandfather had started just after the first World War. Instead, I accepted an offer to fill in for a sick professor and teach at a Swiss university for one year. From there I moved to a job with a Swiss pharmaceutical company and began traveling the world. Five years later, I became director of a business advisory group based in Dusseldorf, Germany. I had to leave the US, and all the traditions and celebrations I was used to, in order to discover a new life, and new traditions.

It was in Europe I took the mind-boggling step and began writing fiction on the side. Nine years and seven books later, my first manuscript was finally accepted for publication by Bethany House...now a division of Baker, a company that was also publishing great books from this unknown writer and speaker out in California by the name of Laura Walker. She would write some bestselling nonfiction, would later win awards for her fiction, and I thought her writing (and her sense of humor) were wonderful.

Fast forward thirty-five years. I am back in England, serving as writer-in-residence at one of the colleges of Oxford University, where my wife has taught law for over thirty years.

The thing is, I never went home. This vagrant's life has meant I've celebrated Christmas in over two dozen countries. I do make it back to the States at least once every year, but very seldom does this mean I can have an American-style Christmas. And so it happened that, until I began reading this wonderful book, I had forgotten just what a special and memorable time Christmas at home truly is.

Laura Walker is a wonderful writer, and every reader of her remarkable book should enter with an open heart, a happy spirit, and if possible a cup of spiked eggnog. Each chapter becomes a recipe for gladness, a quilting together of who we are as a nation, what we share in common, and how we bind ourselves together in spirit and celebration at this unique point each year.

What Ms. Walker captures most eloquently of all, however, are the universal themes of this most majestic of seasons. Tradition, family, love, reverence, gratitude all sing in harmony from these glorious pages. And hope most of all.

For myself, reading these pages have been a mirror. Who I am, what I have missed in the transforming path of life, how special it is to be at home and laughing and rejoined with family in any season. But most especially at Christmas. As you read this book, you'll remember how special this season is.

Wishing you and yours a very merry Christmas season,

—Davis Bunn

Davis Bunn is the author of *A Sea Glass Christmas, The Christmas Cottage, The Christmas Hummingbird, Tidings of Comfort and Joy*, and the entire "Miramar Bay" series of books. He has sold more than eight million copies of his books worldwide, in twenty-six languages, had numerous bestsellers, and won Best Book of the Year numerous times. He and his wife live in Henley-on-Thames, England.

Introduction

*Selfishness makes Christmas a burden;
love makes it a delight.*
—Author Unknown

Christmas is my favorite holiday. My husband's, too. I'm married to "Mr. Christmas." I've never known anyone who loves Christmas as much as Michael. A talented artist and a true Renaissance man, my husband goes all-out for the holiday.

And doesn't break the bank doing so.

It's easy to get caught up in the holiday fever and spend more money than you'd planned (been there, done that) buying gifts not just for loved ones, but for everyone you've ever met. Or buying the biggest, best artificial tree every few years to replace the old artificial tree that doesn't have as many bells and whistles. Perhaps you're determined to rival Clark Griswold's light display in *National Lampoon's Christmas Vacation*. Whatever your Christmas weakness, maybe we could all take a lesson from *Miracle on 34th Street*.

There's a great line in that beloved 1947 classic where Kris Kringle is talking to teenage Alfred, who sweeps the floors at Macy's. As Kris bemoans that Christmas has become so commercial, Alfred agrees, saying in his great New York accent, "Yeah, there's a lot of bad isms floating around this world, but one of the woist is commoicialism."[1]

Alfred goes on to say that people are forgetting what Christmas stands for.

Exactly. Let's not let "commoicialism" rob the joy from Christmas. Instead, why don't we find ways to make the season bright by implementing the Golden Rule of: *"doing unto others as we would have them do unto us."* As Charles Dickens said, let's "honour Christmas in my heart, and try to keep it all the year."[2]

Within these pages, I'll share ways for you to enjoy this most wonderful time of the year with ideas and activities—both sacred and secular—as well as thoughts and stories from my life and others', along with recipes, tips, and quotes.

I love quotes, like this one from Edna Ferber: "Christmas isn't a season. It's a feeling."

It's my desire to inspire you to see Christmas from a slightly different vantage point. Whether you more resemble the Grinch or one of the magi from the East, I hope that this book will help you increase your celebration, internally and externally.

Keep in mind that Christmas is so much more than just a tree, decorations, the church pageant, shopping, and (ugh) fruitcake. Christmas celebrates the birth of Jesus, the one who came to give us new life.

---

1. *Miracle on 34th Street*, directed by George Seaton (Twentieth Century Fox, 1947).
2. Charles Dickens, *A Christmas Carol* (J. M. Dent & Sons LTD, 1921), 137.

> He lies in a manger,
> Ruler of the stars,
> He nurses at his mother's breast,
> He is both great in the nature of God,
> And small in the form of a servant.
> —Augustine of Hippo

1

Merry Yuletide Journey

> *The way you spend Christmas is far more important than how much.*
> —Henry David Thoreau

Whether you are married or single, with kids or without, there are many ways to make the season bright.

One holiday season some friends of ours decided not to put up a Christmas tree, lights, or any decorations. After all, it was just the two of them, no kids; they thought, "Why bother?"

Why indeed.

Even though it's just Michael, me, and our darling rescue dogs, Peanut and Poppy, we still decorate. It's a tradition, and traditions are important to our health and well-being. In addition to helping us understand how we fit into a given special day or season, they also help us through the hard times. When life is uncertain or the road is difficult, there is comfort and continuity in doing things the way we've always done them.

Sometimes our friends marvel at the amount of "stuff" we put out at Christmas. It's true; we do have a lot of decorations. But it's much more than just "stuff." It's memories—reminders of years and decades past. And the people we love(d). Like the nativity scene Michael's mother made for him ages ago. The artificial tree his mom and sister bought in the mid-1970s—it still looked great when decorated. (Up until last year, that is, when it finally gave up the ghost.) The hand-carved wooden ornaments from my air force days in Germany.

Then there are the years we've shared, as well—moments that might have been forgotten were it not for the associated mementos. Each year, as we unpack our Christmas boxes, we are reminded of our history and our heritage.

The first Christmas after my mom died, I saw a beautiful ornament in our local hardware store of a Victorian girl ice-skating and bought it in remembrance of her. Mom and I shared a love of pretty, "girly" things—I inherited the decorating gene from her. This ornament also reminded me of Midwestern winters when we were little and Mom would take us ice-skating at the neighborhood pond. Every year now, when I put this pretty Victorian skater on the tree, I'm reminded of my mother and those halcyon days of childhood in Racine, Wisconsin.

Since my parents worked, Dad's mom, Grandma Florence, would watch my sister and me in the afternoons after school. Lisa and I would trudge through the snow to Grandma's house in our red rubber snow boots, pink-cheeked and bundled up against the cold in our winter coats, woolen hats, and mittens. At Grandma's, we'd shed our boots and pull on a pair of warm Muk Luks—woven slippers with leather bottoms—she kept at the house for us. Then we'd settle in the kitchen with mugs of warm cocoa and homemade cookies fresh from the oven. (Like Sheldon from *The Big Bang Theory* always said about his Meemaw, her cookies were the best!)

After we finished our cocoa and cookies, Grandma would set us up with TV tables in the living room to work on a Christmas craft project. She'd pull out boxes of glitter, felt, rickrack, and sequins from her crafting stash, along with bottles of Elmer's glue, so that we could make ornaments for our parents. One year, she even taught us how to make a Christmas tree from an issue of *Reader's Digest*. Grandma showed us how to take the top corner of each magazine page and fold it so that the corner met the binding, thus forming a sort of triangular shape. Once all the pages were folded, we'd fasten the front and back covers together with the top and bottom of the magazine with a paper clip to make it three-dimensional. We'd then spray paint our creations green, gold, or silver, add a star to the top, and—voilà—instant Christmas trees!

Christmas Eve, Grandma served our family traditional Norwegian lutefisk, a stinky, lye-soaked, dried fish refashioned into a jelly-like substance that *no one* (apart from my dad and grandparents) liked. For the rest of us, Grandma Florence made King Oscar *Fiskebollers* (fish balls)—a combination of haddock, white fish, and cod, pulverized and somehow mysteriously held together to form a slippery ball the size of a walnut. (Researching the ingredients, I learned fish balls are held together with tapioca starch, milk powder, spices, salt, and a trace of canola oil. Grandma always served her fish balls in a mustard gravy with mashed potatoes and peas, but since I hate peas, I'd always hide the little green balls beneath the rim of my plate.)

Afterward, we'd head to the Christmas Eve service at church, where my sister and I would sing in the cherub choir, high up in the balcony, trying not to fall asleep.

On Christmas morning, we'd wake up and race downstairs to see all the presents beneath the tree. We'd be itching to tear into the packages, but we had to wait until Mom and Dad joined us, coffee cups in hand. I'll never forget the year Dad bought this great children's play tunnel, made of polka-dotted fabric stretched over what looked like a giant Slinky. On Christmas Eve, while we slept, Dad set up the tunnel at the base of the stairs.

We woke up Christmas morning and took the stairs two at a time to see what Santa had brought. But at the bottom of the stairs, something barred our way. Lisa and I giggled as we crawled through this fun and unexpected tunnel to reach the rest of our presents.

A Christmas I'll never forget.

Yet as we grow and merge families through marriage, some traditions change or disappear altogether. Every newlywed feels the clash when they hear their spouse say, "That's not the way *my* family does it." And so, the traditions change. Whether it's doing things the way your spouse always did them growing up, or deciding on new ways to celebrate, your traditions can still bring you together at Christmas.

One free, fun, and flexible thing to do during the holiday season is to drive around looking at Christmas lights in different neighborhoods.

Every year, our local newspaper publishes a special section with maps of the areas that have gone the extra kilowatt with their outdoor decorating. For years, there was one street we liked to visit in a suburb about a half-hour's drive away. Complete with traffic directors, all cars were instructed to turn off their headlights. (With a speed limit of about five miles per hour, there's not much danger. Besides, with all the lights on the houses, who needs headlights to see?) This court had fabulous decorations, and not just lights. There were life-size figures of the holy family, angels, Santa Claus, and, once, even Elvis. It was better than the Main Street Electrical Parade at Disney theme parks. Some homes are reverent, some fanciful, some beyond tacky in their exuberance. (Clark Griswold had nothing on them.)

As someone who's more drawn to the classic and traditional, however, overkill and tacky has never been my style. I prefer elegant. That's why, about fifteen years ago, we started going to a different neighborhood in an older, more established part of town where some of the homes date back to more than a century.

I adore old houses—Victorians, and stone or redbrick "cottages" like you might see in England. This neighborhood, known as the "Fab Forties," is an upscale neighborhood with big houses that we could never afford. (When he was governor of California in the 1970s, Ronald Reagan had a home there.)

Real estate is pricey in the Fab Forties, but what I love about this neighborhood is that no two houses are the same, unlike the cookie-cutter homes found in most new developments. Classic wooden colonials, fronted by white columns, nestle alongside two-story, brick English Tudors and large Spanish haciendas with white stucco and red-tile roofs.

During the holidays, traffic slows to a crawl as families and friends gaze wide-eyed at the Christmas splendor on display. Sometimes, we want to take a closer look at specific houses, though, to take it all in. We've been known to park on the main street and walk through the neighborhood instead. One year, as we were walking through the Fab Forties with several friends, we decided to do some impromptu caroling on the sidewalk—in four-part harmony, no less. (Most of us had sung in choirs.) Cars rolled down their windows, and residents came out to listen and join in. One woman even brought us out some hot chocolate to warm us up.

A special moment that could not have been planned.

A couple of miles down the street from us sits one of our favorite decorated houses. A classic, sprawling, two-story brick mansion owned by a well-to-do local developer and his family, this beautiful home, with its classic lines and gabled roofline, looks like something out of a fairy tale. The redbrick home is the epitome of elegance, with white lights running along every line of the two-story structure. Michael has been known to lust after this eye-catching display. He used to wonder how long it took the owner to put up his lights—until he realized that the wealthy developer likely hired his own electrical crew to go up on the housetop.

Michael knows that coveting his neighbor's roofline isn't kosher, so he resigns himself to doing the best he can with what we've got on the basic, rectangular roof of our 1949 ranch house. (A house I've done my best to turn into a wannabe English cottage.) A few years ago, however, Michael got this great little black box from the hardware store that projects a sparkling, laser-light display on the garage door. All he has to do is stick the stake in the ground and turn it on. Easy-peasy.

And no need to get up on a ladder.

2

O Come, All Ye Fruitcakes

Never eat more than you can lift.
—Miss Piggy

I hate fruitcake.* I've hated it my whole life. I submit that the world is divided into two kinds of people: those who like fruitcake—and send it to everyone on their Christmas list—and those who can't abide the heavy, sticky slab of "sweetness" and recycle it to someone else. Someone who likes hard, dry, inedible "cake" with (ugh) gelatinous fruit and nuts inside.

*I'm talking about American fruitcake here. English fruitcake—or traditional "Christmas Cake," as the Brits call it—is moist and flavorful. Made with dried fruits like currants, sultanas (golden raisins), raisins, and dates; sometimes soaked in brandy, rum, or whiskey for weeks; flavored with cinnamon and nutmeg. English home bakers—and professional ones—often decorate their Christmas cake with marzipan on top, or "royal icing." If you're fans of *The Great British Baking Show*, you'll have heard of royal icing: a hard white icing made from beaten egg whites, powdered sugar, and, occasionally, lime or lemon juice.

The British have many different kinds of fruitcake and various ways of making them. The tradition of Christmas cakes in the UK goes back hundreds of years, to a time when fresh fruit in the wintertime was extremely rare. Dried summer fruits were available, however, and were used to make their holiday treats. Even today, most traditional English Christmas cakes are frosted with marzipan or icing. This was a functional choice, as marzipan allowed the cakes to be made ahead of time and kept them from drying out. Soaking the pre-iced cakes in brandy, rum, or some other alcohol was another method of preserving them.

During the first year of the COVID-19 pandemic, when so many people were baking homemade bread, Michael baked fruitcakes. Many types of fruitcakes. One recipe starts months ahead of time and requires several soakings in alcohol. It tasted good, but he felt all the extra effort was unnecessary. The following is his favorite version and can be made start to finish in just a couple of hours.

*Fruitfully Loaded Spice Cake**

**Renamed for those (like me) who hate fruitcake. This recipe was adapted and Americanized from the elementary school cookbook of our English friend Patricia Smith. Even those who usually don't like "fruitcake" like it this way.

Ingredients:

- 2 cups flour
- 1 tablespoon baking powder
- ½ teaspoon salt
- ½ teaspoon cinnamon
- ¼ teaspoon nutmeg

- ¼ teaspoon ginger
- 10 tablespoons butter
- ¾ cup baker's sugar (see note)
- 2 eggs
- 2 cups mixed dried fruit (see note)
- ½ cup milk, minus 2 tablespoons

Note: Baker's sugar has finer granules than regular white sugar. While baker's sugar is ideal for use in this recipe, granulated sugar works just fine. Use whatever dried fruits you like or have on hand: Raisins, golden raisins, dried cranberries, cherries, apricots, figs, prunes, dates, and so on.

Instructions:

1. Prepare the dried fruit. Raisins, dried cranberries, or blueberries are the perfect size, but you'll want to chop up anything larger, like dried apricots or dates. If the fruit is on the older side, you can plump it up by soaking it in warm water while you gather the other necessary ingredients. Fifteen to thirty minutes should do the trick.

2. Preheat the oven to 300 degrees Fahrenheit. (Yep, 300. It bakes at a lower temperature than most traditional cakes for a longer period of time.)

3. Prepare your cake tin. It should be an 8- or 9-inch round pan. Ideally, line the bottom with a layer of parchment paper, cut to the size of the tin. Generously grease and flour the sides of the tin (or all sides of the tin if you don't use parchment).

4. Sift together the flour, spices, salt, and baking powder. If you don't have a sifter, it's okay to use a fine mesh wire strainer and a spatula. That's what Michael does.

5. In a separate bowl, beat together the butter and baker's sugar until fluffy.
6. Add eggs one at a time, incorporating a couple of tablespoons of the flour mixture with the second egg.
7. Fold the fruit into the fluffy egg mixture.
8. Fold the rest of the flour mixture into the wet mixture. Do this with a handheld spatula, not with an electric mixer. It's important not to overwork the flour.
9. Add milk and fold in until well mixed.
10. Pour finished mixture into your prepared cake pan.
11. Bake for 80 to 90 minutes, until the top is firm and the edges start to release from the sides of the pan.
12. Remove from oven and let rest in the tin for five minutes.
13. Remove cake from tin. Remove parchment and cool on a wire rack.

Although I hate fruitcake, I love almost every other baked good associated with the Christmas season. I especially love those delicious smells coming from the kitchen as those goodies bake. Yum!

Heavenly aromas were always emanating from Grandma Florence's kitchen. Some of my fondest memories of growing up in Wisconsin are of going to Grandma's house. No matter what time of day we visited, the moment the door opened, my child's nose detected a kid's favorite fragrance—cookies, cakes, candy, or pie—wafting through the house. (Grandma even made homemade doughnuts that were so much better than store-bought.)

Grandma Florence was the quintessential old-fashioned grandmother: sweet, plump, with graying hair, and always bustling about in a housedress and apron. My entire life, she wore only skirts and dresses; I never once saw her in pants. (Although a black-and-white photo from back in the day shows her wearing them when she went fishing.)

And, boy, could she bake!

Homemade devil's food cake—sinfully rich—with boiled fluffy white frosting that cracked deliciously when you bit into it; apple pie, rhubarb pie, chocolate cream pie, pumpkin pie, and my dad's pie favorite, lemon meringue; every cookie under the sun, including oatmeal, molasses, chocolate chip, peanut butter, sugar, spritz, and Grandma's famous fattigmans bakkels (pronounced "fut-a-mun buckles.")

Fattigmans are Scandinavian Christmas cookies (some say Danish, some say Norwegian, but Grandma Florence was a Norwegian married to a Dane) of diamond-shaped featherweight dough deep-fried and dusted with powdered sugar. Eating one of these holiday favorites was like biting into air—golden, delicious air with a delicate powdered-sugar crunch that melted in your mouth.

Heaven.

Here's a touch of heaven I'd like to share with you, as passed on to me from my grandmother, in her exact words.

Grandma Florence's Fattigmans Bakkels

Ingredients:

- 1 dozen eggs (9 yolks and 3 whole eggs)
- 12 tablespoons sugar
- 12 tablespoons whipped cream
- ¾ teaspoons cardamom
- About 4 cups flour (not too much)
- 1 teaspoon lemon juice
- 2 tablespoons brandy

- 1 lump of butter the size of a walnut
- Pinch of salt

Instructions:

1. Mix and cream well together (all ingredients except flour) and keep the dough cold to be easily handled. Then add enough flour (a little at a time) to make a soft dough—about 4 cups. Be sure not too much flour.
2. Roll out very thin and cut into diamond shapes. Cut a slit near one end and pull other end through.
3. Deep fry at 370 degrees. Don't fry too hard or keep the grease too hot—just golden color.
4. Drain on paper towels or brown paper.
5. Then, roll in powdered sugar.
6. Remember, not too much flour!

I miss Grandma Florence and her floured thumb—I inherited my sweet tooth from her. What I didn't inherit was her year-round love of baking.

I rarely bake any other time of year—too many deadlines, too little time. Yet, come December, I break out the cookie sheets and prepare for a baking marathon. For years, my mom, my sister, and I would gather on a Saturday in early December—with our favorite recipes and ingredients—and spend the day baking Christmas cookies, accompanied by Christmas music. Occasionally, I'd slip *White Christmas* into the VCR so we could steal glances at Bing Crosby and Rosemary Clooney making goo-goo eyes at each other while the cookies baked. It never failed, though; whenever we got to a good part, bing! The timer would go off, and we'd have to turn our attention back to the oven to remove the cookies before they burned.

My favorite Christmas cookies are peanut butter blossoms (peanut butter cookies with Hershey's Kisses on top). When we were little, our Great-Aunt Lorraine, who was my dad's aunt, first introduced us to this magical combination of peanut butter and chocolate. I fell in love at the first bite. As an added special treat, we got to spend the night at her and Uncle Bob's house in Milwaukee. It's simply not Christmas without peanut butter blossoms. I especially love these cookies warm from the oven when the chocolate kiss is still all soft and melty. M'mm, m'mm good.

When I have the time, I also like making fudge—the Kraft marshmallow kind—without nuts. Yum.

For a few years running, in our annual holiday bake-a-thon, my sister Lisa—sadly, no longer with us—made something called "Buffalo Chips." (*Not* the kind from the Wild West.) Lisa's buffalo chips were made with oats, peanut butter, chocolate chips, M&M's, and Rice Krispies. Mouth-wateringly delicious. (She told us the original recipe called for coconut, as well, but she hated coconut—it always got stuck in her teeth—so she left it out.)

Mom's favorite cookies were pecan dreams, but no one else in the family liked nuts, so she'd make M&M cookies and sugar cut-outs for the kids and grandkids instead. (And, when my brother was alive, Grandma's fattigmans bakkels, which Todd loved.)

One year, Mom skipped preparing these Scandinavian specialties since the process is so time-consuming. When Todd arrived for Christmas dinner, he glanced at the plates of cookies and sent Mom a plaintive look. "You didn't make fattigmans?" he said, pushing out his bottom lip in a pout.

That night, mother and son spent a few happy hours together making my brother's favorite cookies. I like to imagine during this holiday season that Mom and Todd are making fattigmans in heaven and sharing them with the rest of the family.

When they were young, our nieces and nephews required us to make cutouts during our annual baking marathons. We used to make these favorite sugar cookies from scratch, but as our lives got busy and our plates too full, we switched to buying the slice-and-bake cookies from the store, which work just as well.

It's the decorating that's important, and the most fun. We like to spread frosting—usually red, green, yellow, and blue—atop cutout stars and angels, snowmen and Santas, reindeer and Christmas trees, covering them with sprinkles, colored sugars, and confetti dots. The kids love decorating these cookies every year.

Michael is the baker and cook in our family (although I make some mean scrambled eggs). Mr. Christmas especially loves baking at Christmastime. He'll usually make different breads and cakes—banana, pumpkin, cranberry-orange, and carrot—to give as gifts.

Michael makes the world's most incredibly moist carrot cake, without nuts—again, I hate most nuts, especially walnuts—that everyone looks forward to when December rolls around. He's been asked to cater parties on the strength of his carrot cake alone. Mr. Christmas has given me permission to share his carrot cake recipe with you (including the secret frosting ingredient).

Michael's Famous Carrot Cake

Ingredients:

- 3 cups flour
- 2 teaspoons baking powder
- 2 teaspoons baking soda
- 2 teaspoons cinnamon
- 1⅛ teaspoons salt, divided
- 4 eggs, separated

- 2 cups sugar
- 1 cup canola oil (or any light vegetable oil)
- ½ cup applesauce
- 2 cups shredded carrots
- 1 cup crushed pineapple with syrup (approximately half a 14-ounce can)
- 2 tablespoons vanilla (yes, tablespoons)
- 1 teaspoon orange extract
- ⅛ teaspoon salt

Instructions:

1. Separate the eggs into yolks and whites. You'll use everything, just at different times.
2. In a medium-sized bowl, sift together the flour, baking powder, baking soda, cinnamon, and 1 teaspoon salt. No sifter? No problem. Just use a fine mesh strainer and spatula. Then give it a quick stir with a dry whisk to make sure everything is evenly distributed.
3. In a separate bowl (or using your stand mixer), beat the egg yolks until blended.
4. Slowly add the sugar, beating until smooth.
5. Add the wet ingredients (except for the egg whites) and mix until blended.
6. Slowly add the flour mixture until just incorporated, either folding by hand or using the slowest speed on your mixer.
7. In a separate bowl, whisk the egg whites until foamy. Add the remaining ⅛ teaspoon salt and whisk on high speed until the egg whites are stiff but not dry.

8. Gently stir a third of the egg whites into the cake batter until incorporated, then fold in the remaining whites. There is a difference between stirring and folding. If you're not sure about this, Google the term "folding" to find helpful video demonstrations. The technique really makes a difference in the fluffiness of the finished product.

9. Pour into a greased 9-by-13-inch cake pan or several small, greased loaf pans. (If you're planning to give away the carrot cake loaves as gifts, use disposable aluminum loaf pans, preferably with lids.)

10. Bake at 350 degrees for 35 minutes before checking for doneness. Loaves may require longer baking time depending on the size. Let cool before frosting.

Cream Cheese Frosting

Ingredients:

- 12 ounces cream cheese, at room temperature
- 4 tablespoons butter, at room temperature
- 2 tablespoons vanilla
- And now, drumroll...the secret ingredient: 2 teaspoons almond extract
- Food coloring (optional if you'd like to add a festive Christmas color to your frosting)
- 8 cups (32 ounces powdered sugar)

Instructions:

1. Mix the cream cheese and butter until light and fluffy.
2. Mix in the vanilla and almond extracts until incorporated.

3. Add food coloring (if using).
4. Slowly add in the powdered sugar. Beat until thoroughly mixed.
5. Frost the cooled carrot cake(s) and enjoy!

Hint: When we give these cakes as gifts, we usually wrap cellophane around the mini loaves, tie them with a pretty ribbon, and attach a homemade Christmas ornament on the top.

A lifetime ago, before I was married, I got together with some girlfriends from my singles group for a fun evening of Christmas cookie baking. We converged on our friend Janna's apartment, each one bringing the ingredients for the cookies we planned to make.

As the five of us baked and chatted, we thought it would be fun to watch an old movie while we made cookies. Eschewing the standard Christmas movie fare, we chose *The Bells of St. Mary's*, starring Ingrid Bergman and Bing Crosby. The wonderful Ingrid, so luminous in *Casablanca*, played the Mother Superior of a group of nuns teaching at an inner-city school, while Bing reprised his Oscar-winning role of Father O'Malley from *Going My Way*.

We found ourselves enraptured by this feel-good movie, in particular because of a scene where some of the parish schoolchildren rehearse the nativity play. The young boy playing Joseph was a scream. At one point, Joseph, who looked to be about four or five years old, takes the little girl playing Mary—a good four inches taller than he—by the hand and guides her over to a pair of sawhorses standing in for the donkey. Joseph hoists Mary up onto the sawhorses, grunting as he does so.

We all burst out laughing. The laughter continued as Joseph delivered his lines with a special panache. When he learned that he and Mary—soon to give birth to the baby Jesus—could stay in the inn, young Joseph slapped his thigh with delight and said, "Well, glory be!"

We laughed so hard we cried.

So entranced were we by the movie that we forgot what ingredients we'd already added to the cookie batter. The two friends, making sugar cookies, mistakenly substituted salt for sugar. (Either that, or we were crying too hard to read the recipe clearly.) When the cookies came out of the oven, they were inedible. Worst cookies ever. Even Janna's cat refused to eat them.

We threw them out, and one of the girls ran to the store for some slice-and-bake cookie dough.

Well, glory be!

A few years ago, Michael came up with a new and delicious cookie recipe that has become a must-make in our house—Sinkers. Or, as they're more formally known, "Everything but the Kitchen Sink." Similar to my sister's Buffalo Chips from back in the day, Sinkers have oats, chocolate chips, butterscotch chips, coconut, and Raisin Bran—yes, the cereal—all baked together to form a lovely, flat, lacy disc of scrumptiousness. Here's the recipe:

Sinkers (aka Everything but the Kitchen Sink Cookies)

Ingredients:

- 1½ cups flour
- 1 teaspoon baking soda
- 1 teaspoon baking powder
- 1 teaspoon salt
- 1 cup butter
- 1 cup brown sugar
- 1 cup granulated sugar
- 2 eggs
- 2 teaspoons vanilla

- 1 cup old-fashioned oats
- ½ cup chocolate chips
- 1 cup butterscotch chips
- ¾ cup coconut flakes
- 1 cup Raisin Bran cereal
- ¾ cup chopped pecans (optional)

(If you're not a fan of Raisin Bran, consider substituting Rice Krispies. And if you don't like butterscotch chips—unfathomable—you can use M&M's Minis or raisins in place of those golden dabs of goodness. If coconut isn't your thing, try substituting a cup of peanut butter instead.)

Instructions:

1. Preheat oven to 350 degrees.
2. In a medium bowl, sift together flour, baking soda, baking powder, and salt.
3. In a separate, larger bowl, cream the butter, sugar, and brown sugar with a blender until fluffy.
4. Add eggs and vanilla, blending well.
5. Add the dry ingredients (flour mixture) to the larger bowl, folding in until combined.
6. Then add the dry oatmeal, chocolate chips, butterscotch chips, coconut flakes, and Raisin Bran, stirring by hand until all ingredients are combined.
7. Line cookie sheets with parchment paper. Using a melon baller (or a large cookie scoop), scoop the dough—slightly rounded—onto the cookie sheets. Do *not* press to flatten. (The dough will spread into large, flat disks in the oven, so be sure to bake only 10 cookies per sheet.)

8. Bake for 12 to 14 minutes, until the edges turn golden brown. Remove the cookie sheets from the oven and place on cooling racks, where the Sinkers will finish "baking," giving you a nice, crunchy outside and a soft center.

Makes approximately 40 Sinkers.

(By the way, I had Michael vet this chapter since he's the baker in the family—apart from the peanut butter blossoms I bake without fail every Christmas.)

3

Deck the Halls

One of the most glorious messes in the world is the mess created in the living room on Christmas Day. Don't clean it up too quickly.
—Andy Rooney

After writing, decorating has always been my favorite form of creative expression. I love to make my house pretty, particularly at the holidays. And, since I'm married to Mr. Christmas, we pull out all the stops for the season. (Michael doesn't know the meaning of "Less is more.") Not everyone has the decorating gene or an eye for decor, though, and that's okay. You don't have to be Martha Stewart to make your home festive for the holidays.

Our first Christmas together as a married couple—we met in January, Michael proposed in March, and we wed in August—we were living in a tiny apartment that didn't have much decorating room. As a result, we bought an artificial tabletop Christmas tree that year. One late November day, while I was out grocery shopping, Michael decided to surprise me by putting up the tree and beginning to decorate it.

When I walked into our apartment, what to my wondering eyes should appear but colored tree lights blinking Christmas cheer and a construction paper-chain garland looped around the branches? As my gaze traveled upward, I beheld clumps of flashy gold garland draped above the window.

I stopped in my tracks. I've always been more of a simple, white, non-blinking lights kind of girl, and strands of shimmery pearls were my garland of choice. "Oh, you've put up the tree," I managed brightly.

"Yep!" Michael said, beaming as he looked up from his box of ornaments. "Surprised?"

"I'll say."

To recover from the flashy garland and get into the Christmas spirit, I made us mugs of hot chocolate and nestled in among the boxes of ornaments. From his box, Michael pulled out Mickey Mouse, Charlie Brown, and other colorful plastic cartoon characters with delight. Next, like a kid in a candy store, he produced reindeer, snowmen, and fat Santa dough ornaments he'd hand-painted years earlier.

Meanwhile, I gently unwrapped delicate glass balls, dainty white porcelain trinkets in the shapes of teacups, hearts, and angels, along with a variety of other silver-and-gold, often lacy, Victorian-style baubles.

Talk about a taste collision.

We realized that between the two of us, we had far too many ornaments for the little tree, so we democratically decided to each pick our top fifteen ornaments. When we finished trimming the tree, Mickey Mouse snuggled up next to a pink-and-white rose-patterned teacup, while Snoopy, in all his primary-colored Christmas finery, made eyes at my pretty gold-and-lace angel.

Truly a remarkable sight.

The next day, when my beloved got home from work, Mickey, the Peanuts gang, and most of their little cartoon friends had mysteriously migrated to the back of the tree, encircled by the paper chain garland. The front of the tree was now a thing of beauty with symmetrically looped strings of white pearls gleaming behind a host of silver and gold Victorian ornaments.

For some reason, my new husband wasn't happy with this arrangement.

"You hate all my ornaments, don't you?" Michael said.

"Of course not, honey. I just thought it looked better to group all the bright, primary-colored ones in one area and the pretty—uh, I mean *girly*—ones in another. Besides," I added, pointing to the far-right side of the tree, "I kept your favorite Charlie Brown ornament in front."

The following year when we were living in a larger place, we invested in "his and her" trees—later renamed the Victorian tree and the fun tree once I stepped off my snobby pedestal.

My husband is not a typical male. Michael's not a sports guy (thank goodness; sports have never been my thing), a gamer, someone who tinkers with cars, or a couch potato who watches TV 24/7. My Renaissance man is an artist, cook, woodworker, gardener with his own greenhouse, and the most talented and creative person I've ever known.

Michael's a crafty guy. That man can make *anything*—from quilts and wall hangings to paintings and mosaics to tables and theater sets, as well as original stained-glass and fused-glass creations. And ornaments—lots of ornaments. Every year since he was in college—long before I met him—Michael has made a special Christmas ornament to mark the year.

One ornament has special significance.

In the second year of our marriage, when I was going through chemotherapy after surgery for breast cancer, the chemotherapy—and my reaction to it—was so severe that I had to be on intravenous fluids for a week after each infusion. Thankfully, I was able to undergo these treatments at home.

Michael changed my IV bags, gave me shots, and administered my anti-nausea medication, which came in a plastic container, via my IV. Maybe because it was autumn, or maybe because he's simply demented (his words), he noticed that the casing of the anti-nausea medication somewhat resembled an ornament, with its slightly elongated, baseball-sized shape. Michael even observed this ornament wannabe conveniently hung from its own "string" of plastic tubing.

When my husband pointed out this resemblance I didn't find it amusing. The nausea after chemo was so horrible that I couldn't eat anything, which resulted in my losing thirty pounds in thirty days. Not a diet plan I'd recommend. That thing he was dangling in front of me was to prevent me from retching, *not* a Christmas decoration.

But a plan began forming in Michael's mind.

He thought about the stories from the Old Testament of the children of Israel building things and observing practices that would serve as mementos in the future. The Passover celebration is filled with such mementos. During a Seder, special food is eaten in remembrance of God's faithfulness. Holy Communion is the same. Jesus instructed His disciples, *"Do this in remembrance of me"* (Luke 22:19).

Knowing the cancer was a turning point in our lives, one of those things that irrevocably changes us, Michael determined to make a tribute to remind us as the years passed. In a very small way, like the Passover celebration. To remind us of something from which God had delivered us.

When he mentioned wanting to make ornaments out of the "chemo balls," I said, "No way! You're not going to hang that on the tree. You're twisted."

My beloved admitted that this might be the truth, but he could envision what the chemo ball would become when its transformation was complete. I saw only a piece of an IV tube and the plastic container that held the stuff to keep me from throwing up. I wanted no reminder of that.

In Michael's mind's eye, though, he saw it completed as an object of beauty.

Kind of the way God sees us. Not as we were, but as we can and will be.

That year, everyone in our inner circle received one of those chemo-ball ornaments for Christmas, each one beautifully decorated and bearing the recipient's name, as well as the year.

Mine was decorated especially for our Victorian tree, painted white with pearls and eyelet lace and swoops of pink and white ribbons. Michael decorated his with the fun tree in mind, covering the elongated ball with chubby dancing Santas.

For the first few years after finishing my cancer treatment, I insisted that my chemo-ball ornament hang on the back of the tree. I acknowledged its beauty, but it was still too painful to bring forward. Slowly, it worked its way to the front of the tree, a little bit at a time, year by year.

In 2000, the year my book *Thanks for the Mammogram!* came out (a little pink book about coping with breast cancer with faith, hope, and a healthy dose of laughter), I agreed that the ornament deserved to be front and center.

Tree-Trimming Tip

Try introducing some unconventional decorations to your Christmas tree. For instance, our Victorian tree sports some little-girl toy china teacups and an occasional lace doily draped over a branch. The pearl garland on the Victorian tree inspired the garland on the fun tree: Michael's mother's brightly colored bead necklaces clasped together. We received them after his mom died, still in the wooden jewelry box Michael had made for her in ninth-grade shop class.

4

Of Craft Fairs and Homemade Gifts

God loves the person who gives with joy. Whoever gives with joy gives more.
—Mother Teresa

Ask any mom or grandma, and they'll tell you it's often the handcrafted gifts that mean the most. Or ask any big sister, for that matter.

Michael's sister Debbie still has the paper holder he made her way back in ninth-grade shop class. The cheesy wooden duck with a clothespin for a beak. Tilting its head back opens its mouth and releases the papers. No matter how many times Debbie moves homes, the duck paper holder still has a place next to her computer.

Then there's the treasure that hangs in our living room: a three-foot-square framed set of nine antique crazy quilt blocks that had been sitting in the closet of Michael's grandmother Adelaide for years. The blocks were lovingly stitched by Adelaide's grandmother, Flora, from Flora's daughter Mary's little dresses. Mary was Adelaide's mother. The crazy quilt fabrics are beautiful, featuring velvet and satin with intricate hand embroidery.

One year, knowing that Michael liked to quilt, Grandma Adelaide handed him the bag of fabric squares and said, "Maybe you can do something with this."

Since the fabric squares were so old and delicate, Michael knew turning them into a quilt wouldn't be a good idea. Instead, he carefully stitched the ancient squares onto a piece of muslin, stretched the muslin across a piece of backer board, and built a wooden frame to enclose his homage to Adelaide's mother. He added a piece of clear plexiglass to the front to protect the fabric and slipped the finished piece inside the frame. Michael then went to a sign shop and had a small metal plaque made bearing the name of his great-great-grandmother, Flora Shattuck, born in 1862, died in 1940.

Adelaide loved this hand-crafted gift made with love, and cried when she opened it.

After Adelaide died, the framed quilt blocks were returned to Michael and now hang in a place of pride on our living room wall.

I have a similar treasure that means the world to me. My father, whom I adored, died when I was only fifteen. A wonderful artist, in his spare time, Dad was always sketching, drawing, or painting. His mother, my grandmother, an accomplished needleworker in her own right, was justifiably proud of her son's artistic talent.

Grandma Florence was equally proud of her Norwegian heritage. One year, when I was about six or seven years old, she decided she wanted to combine these three loves into a unique work of art. She asked her son, David (my father), to draw her a picture of Norway on a piece of heavy muslin that she would then "paint" with yarn in an ambitious crewel work project. Dad sketched a three-by-four-foot pastoral scene of the Norwegian countryside for his mother, complete with mountains and a stream flowing past a cabin on a hill. In the foreground, a farm girl in traditional Norwegian dress sits in front of the cabin among the sheep and cows.

After Dad gave his mom the completed drawing, Grandma Florence pulled out her colorful embroidery yarn and began stitching. A busy homemaker who made everything from scratch, she'd stitch in between baking, cleaning, cooking for Grandpa Augie, and watching my sister and me after school. I remember seeing Grandma sitting in front of a large wooden frame in the dining room, pushing blue, red, yellow, green, and brown threads through the canvas with a heavy needle. It took her months to complete this crewel work project, but at last it was finished.

Grandpa Augie proudly hung his wife's finished work of art above the dining room buffet, where we could all enjoy looking at it during holiday dinners. After Grandma Florence died, Grandpa Augie remarried, and we moved out West, so this special piece was given to my aunt Kathy. Unfortunately, Kathy didn't have a place large enough in her house to display it, so she, in turn, gave the needlework art to my aunt Sharon. She didn't have a good place to display it, either, so it remained tucked away for years.

One year, when Uncle Jimmy and Aunt Sharon came out to visit, Sharon gave the piece of folded-up fabric, preserved in tissue paper, to my older sister, Lisa, to keep it in the family. Lisa kept this treasure safely tucked away in her closet, always intending to get this family heirloom framed to hang in her apartment.

Unfortunately, that never happened. Sadly, Lisa passed away last year. When we were clearing out my sister's apartment, I found Grandma's crewel work in a bag on a shelf in the closet. I brought it home and asked Michael if he could frame it for me. My creative Renaissance man sewed a fabric border around the edge of this sixty-year-old textile and affixed the border to a wooden frame he made. It now hangs proudly above our bed.

Every time I look at this one-of-a-kind fabric artwork, I think of my dad, my grandma, my sister, my aunts, and cherished holiday dinners at my grandparents' house.

A great homemade gift to make for friends and family is Christmas ornaments. An ornament can be the present itself or an extra-special gift wrap decoration. Michael has been making and giving ornaments for years. Colorful beaded ornaments are his specialty. My husband is one of those people who can't sit still and just watch TV; he has to be doing something. So, as we watch our favorite English mysteries or *Masterpiece Theatre* presentations, he'll pull out wire and his box of beads and start making ornaments.

Michael also has a tradition of making a special ornament each year, always writing the recipient's name and the year on the back of each ornament. The oldest one with his name on it is a bread-dough bell that was shaped by a cookie cutter and painted red with green trim, dated 1979. (Oops, Michael just reminded me this ornament disintegrated a couple of years ago. Sorry about that.)

Sometimes the ornaments are simple, like the first year we attended *The Nutcracker* together. Michael cut the colorful pictures off the program covers, glued them to poster board, and hung them from golden ribbon—one for each of us. He wrote our names and the year on the back as a reminder of the special occasion.

Another year, Michael went to a "pottery lounge" with his work colleagues for a team-building Christmas event. At this paint-your-own pottery place, customers choose a piece of unfinished ceramics, pick their paint colors, then design and paint their piece of art while chatting, listening to music, and sipping tea or coffee. Michael painted two ceramic ball Christmas tree ornaments for us that year—one with a nativity scene, the other a pretty wreath, adding our names and the year on the back. Afterward, he and his coworkers left their ornaments with the staff to be glazed and fired in their ceramic kiln, to be picked up forty-eight hours later.

I loved these unique, one-of-a-kind ornaments my husband made. There's only one problem—those things are heavy! Too heavy for the smaller, artificial tree we got a few years ago. Rather than hanging them on the tree, these days we display them on a bookcase instead.

Since he retired, Michael's gotten involved in a yearly Christmas craft fair. He starts making his creations for the holiday fair months in advance, crafting beaded ornaments and suncatchers or crocheting gorgeous scarves from his recliner while we watch TV together in the evenings.

Over the past couple of years, though, he's added original creations that can't be made from the comfort of his recliner. For these, he retires to his studio—formerly the guest bedroom—to make fused glass pendants, ornaments for Christmas trees, and his latest addition: plant stakes with intricate floral decoration glass toppers fused in his microwave kiln. Michael will also take over the dining room table when he needs more room for his crafting projects. Last year, he snagged some great six-by-eight-inch "signs" made from corrugated metal and hung with twine at the local dollar store to decorate, as well as unpainted wooden cutouts of Santa, snowmen, Christmas trees, winter cottages, and wooden letters spelling out the word "Peace" with a Christmas tree and star in the center. He pulled out his paints and crafting decorations—artificial holly and red berries, sprigs of fake evergreen, chubby Santas, cute snowmen and penguins, sleek reindeer, nativity cutouts, small red velvet bows and ribbons, and assorted holiday sayings like "Ho, Ho, Ho!," "Merry Christmas," "Joyeux Noel," and "Peace on Earth"—and began gluing these festive "ingredients" on top of the metal to create collages that became delightfully whimsical Christmas scenes.

It looked so fun, I wanted to get in on the action. We spent a happy Saturday afternoon together at the dining room table making festive holiday signs on the corrugated metal while listening to Christmas music. (After an hour or two of this, Peanut and Poppy began pawing at our legs, telling us, "Mom and Dad, pay attention to us!")

Michael's favorite sign includes a 3D Santa face and a wooden cutout of the word *Believe*. The one I love features the word *Noel* taking up half the sign with a sprig of evergreen and red berries in the top left-hand corner. Simple and elegant.

When it came time to paint the wooden cutouts, I told Michael I wanted to help with that as well. I had a blast painting three cutouts—a cute Santa, Victorian Christmas cottage, and one of the Peace signs. Then I was done. I ceded my paint brush to the master craftsman and left to make a cup of tea and snuggle in with a good book.

One of my husband's recent holiday craft projects I fell head over heels for were the hand-poured candles in fun mugs and vintage china teacups he picked up for a song at estate sales. I accompanied him to a couple of these sales and called dibs on a few of the prettiest floral teacups, so he set them aside for me.

Michael melts beeswax for these homemade candles in his studio microwave and pours the wax into china cups and mugs, adding essential oils to give them a pleasing scent. He uses lavender, rose, honeysuckle, and plumeria, which, while it may be unfamiliar to many people, gives off a beautiful fragrance when the candle is lit. Other scents include different mints and citrus fruits, including bergamot—used to give Earl Grey tea its distinctive flavor. There are times when there's not enough oil to scent a batch of candles, so he'll will mix the oils, creating a unique aromatic blend. For instance, on one occasion he mixed various scents and named it Orchard Breeze. He's nothing if not creative.

After he finished his first batch of candles, Michael called me into the kitchen to show off his creations. "What do you think?" he asked.

"They're beautiful," I breathed. Pointing at one after another of the English china teacups, I said, "I want *that* one, and *that* one, and *that* one."

"These are to sell at the craft fair, honey."

"I know, but I'm your wife. I get first pick." (Vintage floral teacups are one of my favorite things.) I suggested he go to the thrift shop and buy some more modern and contemporary teacups. "A lot of people like modern," I pointed out.

Not me.

I now have nearly a dozen gorgeous vintage teacup candles scattered around the house—from England, Bavaria, Japan, the US, and Russia. When it comes to beautiful teacups, I don't discriminate as to their origins.

Another lovely and inexpensive gift to give friends and family is a basket of a few of the recipient's favorite things. Whether it's seed packets and a pair of garden gloves for the gardener in your life, assorted teas and coffees or packets of hot chocolate and homemade cookies for the foodie, or batches of fudge and candy for someone with a sweet tooth. One year, when I was working in the marketing department of a private foodstuffs company that specialized in high-end tomato products, we gave baskets of gourmet spaghetti sauce, colored Christmas tree-shaped pasta, and breadsticks for a yummy edible gift to all of our sisters- and brothers-in-law.

Another great idea is to mix up the dry ingredients of your favorite homemade cookie in a Mason jar with a pretty piece of fabric ruffled out of the lid, then attach the recipe to the jar with a colorful ribbon.

After he retired, Michael decided it was time to learn new skills. He took a glass fusing workshop at a local glass store and fell in love. He now has two kilns in his studio that fit in a dedicated microwave where he can melt glass and fuse it together. The first items he made were fused-glass pendants, then he graduated to ornaments. Favorite fused-glass ornaments have been snowmen, and Christmas tress—both elegant, and whimsical.

He also took stained glass lessons at a local glass shop and surprised the instructor at how fast he caught on. He quickly began taking on projects that were considered way too complicated for beginners.

One of my favorite stained-glass creations my Renaissance man made last year is a floral glass "valance" hanging in the kitchen window. Michael made beautiful stained-glass flowers to represent the four seasons: yellow daffodils for spring; a perfect red rose for summer, a pink camellia for winter, and a golden sunflower for fall. Each flower is trimmed in cobalt-blue glass to complement our blue-and-white kitchen and fastened to hooks with chains.

I love my one-of-a-kind glass valance. As do our guests. (Some friends have even commissioned Michael to make them a single stained-glass flower for their window.)

One year, a friend of ours found himself with an extra scroll saw. Promising he would use it to make all kinds of things, Michael persuaded me to buy the saw for him as an early Christmas present. Later that month he gave a wonderful cutout of Joseph and Mary with the baby Jesus in the stable to the friend who sold us the scroll saw.

The following November, Michael noticed the scroll saw in the garage and remembered telling me how much he'd use that gift—which hadn't been turned on in nearly a year. Thinking quickly, he grabbed some pieces of pine and patterns he'd found long ago. He whipped out another nativity scene, this one in a "primitive" style that he figured he'd be able to paint quickly and give to several friends and family members as gifts that year. After all the sanding, marking of the lines, and painting, Michael realized this was not something to be mass-produced.

"I don't remember painting taking so much time," he told me.

I'm not crafty like my husband. Whenever people come over to our house, they ooh and aah over all the beautiful things Michael has made—quilts, oil paintings, stained glass creations, and more—marveling at his talent. After they finish complimenting him, I pipe up, "I'm not crafty. All I do is write and decorate."

Figuring out the perfect way to display things to their best advantage is something I love to do. I enjoy creating tableaus with antique books, china, framed family pictures, and souvenirs from our trips abroad on the fireplace mantel, buffet, corner cupboard, and myriad bookcases throughout the house. (With everything angled just so.)

For our second Christmas together, the year of my cancer, I was too sick to go shopping in the stores. My immune system was so compromised by the heavy-duty chemotherapy treatments, I rarely went out in public, let alone had the energy to walk very far. I've always been one to look at what I *can* do, however, rather than feeling limited by what I can't do. I was determined to make Michael a Christmas present.

I may not craft, but I can write. That year, I wrote a poem for my husband, revised the lyrics to a song we both loved, and added some quotes especially appropriate to us. I bound these writings together in a simple green booklet and gave it to Michael for Christmas.

He loved his gift. In his words, "So much better than socks or a tie."

Handcrafting Tip

If, like me, you're not really the crafty type, yet you feel an urge to "make" a gift for someone special on your Christmas list, pay a visit to your local craft store. You'll find all kinds of kits for various projects that even the beginner or those with very little time to spare can complete and enjoy.

And if making something simply isn't your thing, but you appreciate handcrafted items, visit a craft fair instead and buy someone else's handiwork. That way you're supporting a local artist and giving a one-of-a-kind gift to someone special on your Christmas list. A win-win for everyone!

5

Those Not-so-Silent Nights

That's the magic of art and the magic of theatre. It has the power to transform an audience, an individual, or en masse, to transform them and give them an epiphanal experience that changes their life, opens their hearts and their minds and the way they think.
—Brian Stokes Mitchell

In our house, the Christmas season just isn't complete without our attending some kind of live performance. As I write this in the waning days of December, with Christmas only a few days away, I'm rememberingly fondly the annual Lessons and Carols event we attended at church last Sunday.

It's our favorite service of the year.

This seasonal service is made up of Christmas hymns, lessons (readings from Scripture), and carols sung by our wonderful chancel choir. One of my favorite "carols" is "All My Heart This Night Rejoices" by Z. Randall Stroope. When we were in choir, Michael and I always loved performing this beautiful piece with our choir family. This year, as we sat in the congregation, I closed my eyes as the choir sang the sacred song, thrilling as their sweet, angelic voices soared to the rafters. Glorious. Gave me goose bumps.

Other favorite carols during our Episcopal church service included the ancient chant "Veni, Veni, Emmanuel," "The Song of Mary—Magnificat," and "The Coventry Carol." There is nothing like the sound of a wonderful choir joining their voices together and singing in harmony.

Beautiful.

The congregation joined with the choir to sing such beloved hymns as "Lo, How a Rose e'er Blooming," "Angels We Have Heard on High," and "O Come, All Ye Faithful." After the rector gave a closing blessing, we all stood and ended the evening with "Hark! The Herald Angels Sing," filling me with joy and goodwill. What a treat to be a part of such a wonderful Christmas performance.

My beloved and I sang in the church choir for several years, until, unfortunately, multiple writing deadlines (me) and health issues (Michael) forced us to bow out. I loved singing the melodies of these holy songs with my fellow sopranos, many of whom had studied music for years.

I don't read music, though, and I struggle with math, so I had difficulty counting: 4/4-time, 2/4-time, and 6/8-time. I'd wing it instead; always keeping a vigilant eye on our choir director, listening carefully to the two longtime sopranos flanking me, and making sure to copy them. Somehow, it worked.

One of the things I loved about choir was singing in so many different languages—languages that were unfamiliar to me, particularly Latin. The only Latin phrases I knew were "Carpe diem" and "Veni, vidi, vici." During the annual Lessons and Carols service preceding Christmas, I loved singing "Joyeux Noel," and "Quittez, Pasteurs," in French, and the moving "Magnificat" in

Latin. The beauty of Latin and the sacred, reverent music we sang deeply touched my soul, and they continue to do so to this day.

At the other end of the song spectrum, there's "Adam lay i-bounden/Deo gracias" from Benjamin Britten's *A Ceremony of Carols*, a song based on a fifteenth-century Middle English poem. As an avid Anglophile, I love most things English, but this Middle English piece was not my cup of tea.

Enough said.

In my early twenties, while stationed in England in the air force, I performed in a traditional English pantomime, commonly referred to as "panto" by the British. The Christmas panto is usually a much-loved children's story—*Cinderella*, *Peter Pan*, *Aladdin*, and so on—during the holidays, with a woman playing the "principal boy" character à la Mary Martin or Cathy Rigby in *Peter Pan*.

As the lone American in the theater company of a small English village near the base, I was gobsmacked when I learned I'd won the lead role of Aladdin in the Christmas pantomime! (I'd never even seen a traditional English panto at this point, so it was all a bit strange to this girl from Wisconsin by way of Phoenix.)

Initially, it felt odd to be playing a boy in tights. (My British roommate, Liz, who'd also been cast in the production, explained that traditional panto always includes a woman in tights and high heels playing the principal boy character, and a man in drag playing the Dame.) My costume as Aladdin consisted of a thigh-length Mandarin jacket, black tights, heels, and lots of stage makeup. I threw myself into the role with gusto, trying to look appropriately smitten when, as the principal boy, I had to sing a love song to the teenage princess.

On opening night, all was going well until I uttered the line, "Uncle, where's the lamp?" in my nasally Midwestern accent. By that time, I'd lived in the UK for a couple of years and had picked up a bit of an English accent. I'd gotten into the habit of saying "toe-mah-toe" for tomato, "poe-tah-toe" for potato, and "ack-shualy" for actually. I was also saying expressions like, "I'll ring you up" ("I'll call you") and "Would you like a bit of bread?" rather than offering a "piece" or a "slice" of bread. These English phrases and pronunciations had become part of my daily lexicon.

There were still a few words, however, that I couldn't say the way the Brits did without feeling pretentious, including "al-loo-min-ium," "shed-yule," and—you guessed it—"lahmp."

Saying "lahmp" sounded so to-the-manor-born, which I most assuredly wasn't. On my lips, the word sounded artificial and forced. As well, *Aladdin* was a tale from the Middle East, so an English accent wasn't a prerequisite. Unfortunately, when I said, "Uncle, where's the lamp?" the last word came out "la-a-a-a-amp," which got the biggest unintended laugh of the evening.

What can I say? You can take the girl out of Wisconsin, but you can't take Wisconsin out of the girl.

Over the years, we've attended *The Nutcracker* a handful of times during the holidays. The first time we attended this classic ballet together as a couple, we accompanied Michael's sister Sheri and her family. Michael and I usually like to sit in the balcony for shows with a lot of dancing—that way, we get a great view of the whole stage and the "big picture." At Sheri's suggestion, though, this time we sat close, just three rows from the stage.

Our vantage point was a perfect place to observe the dancers' expressions and the intricate details of the sets and costumes. By sitting so close, we noticed other things as well. One young male dancer was having a lot of trouble with the lifts. We could see the strain on his face as he hoisted a ballerina over his head again and again. As we were walking back to the car after the performance, my sister-in-law remarked, "Bless his heart. He's just not built big enough for all those moves."

Since Michael and I love choral music, we've attended the Christmas concert put on by a prestigious local choir made up of fifty singers, ages eighteen and up, several times over the years. This group of professionally trained singers, sometimes accompanied by a harpsichord and string quartet, kicks off their holiday concert with a candlelight processional in a darkened church by singing a baroque piece or sacred hymn.

Giving me chills every time.

They'll often include an original piece of music I've never heard before, in addition to the gorgeous "Huron Carol" and such crowd-pleasers as "I Saw Three Ships" and "Jingle Bells," which leave the audience smiling and tapping their feet.

Another church performance we'll never forget was when Michael's niece Jennie performed in her church Christmas musical. She played the part of Mary and sang her first solo, "Breath of Heaven," popularized by Amy Grant.

Perfection.

Jennie, seventeen years old at the time, had no vocal training. And she nailed it. Michael, her proud and admittedly biased uncle (who *has* had vocal training), thought she sang it even better than Amy. I agree. Jennie *was* Mary, a teenage girl, not yet a woman, nervous because she was in unfamiliar territory, outside of anything she'd ever experienced. Singing alone for the first time in front of hundreds of people, Jennie too was in unfamiliar territory. Her nervousness enhanced the performance and allowed us to experience how Mary might have felt in Bethlehem, giving birth to the Son of God. My eyes filled, and Michael wept through the entire song. To this day, he still tears up at the memory.

Thanks, Jennie, for stepping out of your comfort zone and giving us a performance we'll never forget.

Our friends Ella and Ryan always try to plan an outing to a festive show during the season, whether it's Tuba Christmas, Lessons and Carols, a performance of the Messiah, or Celtic Christmas.

We've gone to the Celtic Christmas performance at church a few times over the years, and the acoustic band of fiddler, piper, guitarist, and mandolin player made us feel as if we were back in the UK. The group had us all clapping along to the Irish and Scottish tunes, stomping our feet in concert with the classic Irish step dancers in traditional garb.

Our footwork wasn't as intricate as theirs, though.

Show Tips (from Michael, an actor and singer for many years)

No live performance is complete without an audience. One director I worked with even called the audience "the final cast member." Even if you are not a performer, you can still be part of the show. Call up a friend and order some tickets to a local Christmas performance. Adding dinner before or dessert afterward makes for a fun and memorable, albeit not-so-silent, night.

6

Here Comes Doggy Paws, Here Comes Kitty Claws

> *Until one has loved an animal a part of one's soul*
> *remains unawakened.*
> —Anatole France

Parents love hearing the pitter-patter of little feet around the house. We do too—although the pitter-patter in our house is the click-click-click of paws on hardwood floors.

We're dog parents of two canine children.

Diagnosed with breast cancer the day after our first wedding anniversary, I received a heavy-duty course of chemotherapy after my mastectomy to combat this aggressive cancer. Still "newlyweds," Michael and I hadn't yet decided whether or not to have children. There was no rush—after all, we'd only been married just over a year, and I was in my mid-thirties.

As I was finishing chemo, we asked my oncologist about the prospect of our having children someday. He advised us to wait at least five years. There was the chance that cancer cells might still be lurking in my body, and getting pregnant would cause those cells to grow. Waiting five years, though, would put me in my early forties. Back in the day—more than thirty years ago—to me, that seemed too old to become a mom.

It was a different time.

Instead, I became a dog mom, and I loved it. Dogs add a whole new dimension of joy to the holidays that I'd never known before. Dogs add a whole new dimension of joy to *life*.

Our first canine "child" was an American Eskimo named Gracie. Although Michael grew up with dogs running in and out of his house, I'd never had a dog before. So, I made up a list of what I wanted, and didn't want: no big dogs (not enough room in our small house for them, plus their wagging tails might break one of my china teacups); no Chihuahuas (too nervous and yippy; plus, I preferred fluffy dogs, not short-haired ones); no dogs allowed on the furniture—especially the bed. I wanted a medium-sized, friendly, cinnamon-colored dog that didn't bark too much.

Five years into our marriage, one morning we woke up and said, "Let's go find a dog today!"

We started at the local pound looking for just the right dog, then moved on to various animal shelters. At the last shelter we visited, we were checking out a Chow Chow, the perfect cinnamon color I wanted, that looked like a teddy bear. The Chow was bigger than I wanted, though, which I said aloud to Michael.

A woman next to us piped up, "I have a little white spitz that might interest you."

I thought to myself, "White? I don't want a white dog. That's not on my list."

The woman was with a rescue group that had recently rescued this little dog found running wild. She brought out the small spitz, calling her a "sweetheart." She said she'd love to keep the dog herself, but the pup didn't like cats, and she had two cats.

Cuddling the quivering ball of white fur to his chest, Michael gave me a look. A look that told me he'd already fallen hard.

The rescue group lady told us we could take the spitz—originally named German Spitz, the breed was renamed American Eskimo during World War I—home on a trial basis to see if she was a good match. In the car, I held the trembling little white dog on my lap so Michael could drive while I tried to soothe and reassure her. She promptly threw up on my foot.

And in that moment, I became a dog mom.

Our first Christmas with Princess Grace Elizabeth, aka Gracie—two months after bringing her home from the rescue shelter—we gave her some upscale doggy bones and a squeaky toy as Christmas gifts.

Never having had a dog before, I wasn't sure about the whole presents thing. "For a dog?" I thought. "Seriously?"

Gracie wasn't just a dog, though; she was a member of our family. And Michael, who's had several dogs as pets, knows canine creatures better than me. He insisted Gracie would get her feelings hurt if she didn't get something while we were opening our gifts Christmas morning.

"Feelings hurt?" I had a lot to learn about pets.

Michael was right. Dogs do have feelings. Whenever Gracie was sad or worried, we could always tell because she did her "seal pup" impression. With her fluffy creamy fur, she resembled a little white fox with her black nose, big dark eyes, and pointed ears. Ears with a mind of their own, they stood up.

If we scolded Gracie, or if she was unhappy about something, her ears would go straight back and down, making her look like a baby harp seal. Since we didn't want any seal-pup sadness at Christmas, Gracie got a couple of presents every year on the holiday.

We'd stuff Gracie's toys in gift bags—sans tissue paper—and set the bags in front of her. She would knock each bag over, poke her little head inside, and root around until she found her new stuffed animal, which she'd grab victoriously in her mouth.

Such fun.

Occasionally, though, Gracie thought *our* presents were hers. Like the year Michael gave me overstuffed Winnie-the-Pooh slippers. Gracie watched expectantly, a possessive gleam in her eye as I unwrapped the fuzzy gold-and-red slippers. The second I set the slippers down, Gracie lunged for "her" gift, fastened her teeth on one of Pooh's ears, and tried to drag my new footwear away.

"No, no, Gracie," Michael said, "that's Mommy's slipper."

"Huh? But you always give me the animal toys," Gracie must have been thinking.

Michael waved a stuffed lamb under her nose invitingly. "This is your present, Gracie. See? The baa-baa lamb squeaks. Mommy's slippers don't."

Gracie's ears perked up. She looked from Michael to me, and then to her new toy. Dropping the quiet Winnie-the-Pooh, she sprang for the noisy little lamb instead, squeaking to her heart's content.

Our second rescue dog, Mellie, a beautiful spaniel mix we named for the gentle and ladylike "Miss Mellie" in *Gone With the Wind*, was much more mellow than Gracie. The first time we set a Christmas bag in front of Mellie with a toy inside, she glanced at the bag, looked at us, then ambled away. We took the toy out of the bag and held it out to her. She ignored it.

It wasn't until we pressed on the stuffed hedgehog's stomach through the bag, activating the squeaky toy within, that she took notice. Mellie bounded back, grabbed the hedgehog from the bag, and squeaked away.

Such a princess.

My friend Lonnie and her husband, Joe, had a couple of fur princesses in their house too—of the kitty-cat variety. Kit-Kat and Lucy ruled the roost in Joe and Lonnie's Michigan farmhouse. Photos of these feminine felines graced the Christmas tree inside some lovely wooden ornaments Joe bought for Lonnie one year. Lest you think the cats were selfish, though, those kitty-cats knew proper etiquette. At Christmastime, they sent Kit-Kat candy bars to everyone as presents.

Gracie liked to give gifts to her canine and feline family members as well as her neighborhood friends. It started out small with her giving treats to her kitty cousins—Michael's sister's cats, my mom's Chihuahua mix, and the entire canine gang over at Great-Grandma Adelaide's. But then Gracie felt bad about not giving a gift to her friend Jake across town, who'd given her something, and Haley, her Golden Retriever pal across the street.

We added them to the list.

The year that Michael assembled Christmas packages for every one of Gracie's neighborhood pals, and the two of them trotted off happily to deliver them, however, I put my foot down.

When they returned from their mission, I said, "Twenty-two dog presents is too much!"

Two months after our beloved Mellie crossed the Rainbow Bridge, leaving our house feeling so empty, we did something unexpected. We got *two* rescue dogs. Michael thought it might be a good idea to get two dogs at once, giving them both a constant playmate. We'd been looking online for a while when I spotted the photo of a little scruffy-looking dog with big, dark eyes named Poppy that called out to me.

We called the rescue place, and the owner told us Poppy had bonded with another small dog, a terrier mix named Peanut. She sent us Peanut's picture, and we laughed out loud. The little pup reminded us of Max from How the Grinch Stole Christmas. We arranged a time for her to bring both dogs over to the house so we could meet them.

We had established specific guidelines for getting a dog. There were specific things we did *not* want: no male dogs. (They lift their legs and mark their territories.) No puppies. (Too much work, and they get into everything.) No short-haired dogs. (Mellie and Gracie were both pretty, long-haired dogs with soft, lush fur that I loved to brush.) And, last but not least, no Chihuahuas. (Still too yippy in my mind.)

Well.

When we met him, Peanut was nine months old and all puppy. Male, short-haired, and a Chihuahua mix. Also, Poppy's best friend.

From the moment these two pups arrived, they claimed our house as their own. As we watched them frolic and play together, it filled our hearts with joy and our home with laughter. We knew we couldn't split them up. We tossed all our doggie "no's" out the window and went for it. We're so glad we did.

We adore these two little "terror-iers," as we've nicknamed them. Kidlets. Cutie-pies. Snuggle-buddies. The Walker snack-pack: Popcorn and Peanut. We can't wait to give them their stuffed toys and treats on Christmas morning.

Knowing them, they'll tear those gift bags apart in two seconds flat.

Tips on Pet Presents

Maybe you're not one of those people who go overboard with presents for your pet at Christmas. Not a problem. Keep it simple—your four-footed friend will likely be happy with an extra treat. For fun, we've adopted the habit of having our dogs give *us* a present on Christmas. If you need an idea for a gift from a pet, consider a book on animal psychology or any pet-related book. One year, Gracie got Michael a book on why dogs are better than cats.

Tips on Pets as Gifts

What's cuter than a new puppy or kitten under the Christmas tree? They're so adorable, who wouldn't enjoy receiving this snuggly bundle of love?

Tread carefully. Owning a pet is not something to be taken lightly—it's a ten- to twenty-year commitment with ongoing expenses and daily responsibilities. The ASPCA (American Society for the Prevention of Cruelty to Animals) cautions that thousands of unwanted animals wind up in shelters every year.[3]

Many factors should be considered before buying a pet for someone: breed (temperament), size, personality, and age of the animal. Is the potential pet a good match for its intended owner? Also, is December, with all the holiday stress, really a good time to introduce a new member into the household?

Check with your local ASPCA office before making such an important decision.

A great alternative would be to wrap a toy dog or cat for your loved one, along with a "gift certificate" for the real thing. Maybe offer to research what pet would be best for them, then take your friend or family member to the local animal shelter after the holidays, when things have quieted down, to help them find their pet.

---

3. "U.S. Animal Shelter Statistics," Helping Shelters, People and Pets, ASPCA, accessed June 18, 2025, https://www.aspca.org/helping-shelters-people-pets/us-animal-shelter-statistics.

7

Making New Traditions, Breaking Old Traditions

(JUST BECAUSE YOUR FAMILY'S ALWAYS DONE IT THAT WAY DOESN'T MEAN IT'S THE ONLY WAY.)

> *Our hearts grow tender with childhood memories and love of kindred, and we are better throughout the year for having, in spirit, become a child again at Christmastime.*
> —Laura Ingalls Wilder

One of my earliest memories of a childhood Christmas tradition is getting to open one present, and one present only, on Christmas Eve. We didn't get to choose from the selection of gaily wrapped packages underneath the tree, either. Mom did—pajamas. Every year.

What every kid dreams of.

This lone Christmas Eve gift was never a surprise. The annual pj's were always wrapped the same way: rolled up in a tube like a sausage, covered in paper featuring chubby Santas or smiling snowmen on a background of red or green, with curly ribbon tying off each end, and the edges of the paper ruffled like a giant piece of hard candy.

We used to dream that maybe this year it *would* be candy.

Alas, pajamas were the tradition. That's just the way it was. This may have been a tradition for other households back in the day. When Michael and I got married, he told me his mom did the same thing for him and his siblings—pajamas the night before Christmas; even down to the way the pj's were wrapped!

Kindred family spirits.

While Michael's family kept their opening-one-gift-on-Christmas-Eve tradition, he was happy when, somewhere along the line, the pajamas part faded away.

As did the wakeup call at four o'clock in the morning. Every year, one of the six kids in his family would awaken before dawn, too excited to sleep and eager to see what Santa had brought. That child would wake up the rest of the family, and they'd rush to the living room to start the wrapping-paper-ripping frenzy.

Those kids are all grown now with families of their own, so they have changed and adapted their traditions to fit their individual family styles. Michael told me this predawn ritual was one of the first things his sister Sheri changed after she had her twins, Kari and Jennie.

Sheri would warn her daughters: "Don't wake up Mom and Dad until after eight o'clock, under penalty of death. Otherwise, we'll throw away all your new toys."

When his nieces were about nine years old, Michael stayed over at their family's house one Christmas Eve. His bed for the night—the couch—was situated between the girls' room and the tree. At about a quarter to eight, Michael heard little voices in the hallway. He pretended to be asleep while one of the twins elbowed the other. *"Don't* wake up Mika Mike!" (As toddlers, Jennie and Kari couldn't say "Uncle,"—it came out "Mika" instead, a name the twins still call him to this day.) Pretending no more, Michael let Kari and Jennie know that he, too, couldn't wait for Christmas to start.

The eight o'clock tradition was broken that year.

Since we don't have kids, we've never held to any specific "time-to-wake-up" traditions in our marriage. Ours was a whirlwind courtship—we met in January and married in August—so our first Christmas together was *after* our wedding. We learned about each other's family traditions as the season progressed.

A big surprise to me was Michael's family's passion for stocking stuffers. The first, and only, clue arrived Christmas morning. You have to understand that in my family, stockings weren't a big deal, just a nice little addition to the presents under the tree—some pencils, a new toothbrush, little tidbits of this and that, some candy, and a piece of fruit—usually an orange.

So, I filled Michael's stocking accordingly.

Christmas morning, I stared in disbelief at my stocking where it hung from the mantel. Michael had made me a gorgeous new stocking that year: an oversized one in a Victorian style of emerald-green satin with a lace overlay outlined with miniature pearls and trimmed with a garland of rosebud ribbon, fully lined for extra strength. The stocking itself was beautiful, but what really amazed me was how much stuff he had stuffed inside! Perfume, the latest Amy Grant CD, a couple of pairs of pretty earrings, bath salts, miniature scented soaps, and the requisite office supplies: pens, pencils, paper clips, sticky notes, even a box of staples. Not to mention all the chocolate, tea, and tea biscuits, complete with a candy cane sticking out of the top.

And, most importantly, the tangerine in the toe.

His mother always put a tangerine in the toe. Michael and his siblings rarely ate the orange fruit, often sticking it back in the fridge for someone else to eat later. Even so, a stocking without a tangerine in the toe on Christmas morning was unimaginable.

Until my husband forgot to mention this to me.

I don't remember what I put in the toe of my beloved's store-bought, basic red stocking that first Christmas, but it was not small, round, or orange. His stocking was pathetic compared to mine. After all these years, I can't recall exactly what I put in Michael's stocking, but it wasn't much. Probably a new toothbrush, a couple of pencils, and a few pieces of candy.

Major stocking fail.

But how was I to know? My sweetheart's stocking fetish came as a complete surprise, and he's conservative compared to some of his siblings—they make Michael look like Ebenezer Scrooge (before the ghosts).

One year, we finished our holiday preparations early, allowing us time to relax and enjoy the week before Christmas. On Friday evening, thinking it would be fun to spend time with family, we invited Michael's brother Bob and his wife, Debbie, to see the new Sandra Bullock comedy with us. Bob had a meeting that night and couldn't go to the movie. As much as Debbie wanted—and *needed*—to get away, she had stocking stuffers to wrap. We suggested she bring everything over to our house, where the three of us would make light work of the wrapping and still have time for the film.

Good thing there was a late showing that night.

Debbie had goodies for her husband, three sons, one daughter-in-law, two grandchildren, and a few other teens who, although not related by blood or marriage, were still part of the family. The trunk of her car was crammed full of brown paper grocery bags, one bag per person.

"It's the only way to keep it all organized," Debbie explained. Okay, so each bag was only a third full. Still, no wonder she felt overwhelmed by the task of wrapping all that stuff! Especially since she insisted every individual item had to be wrapped.

I stared at my sister-in-law, incredulous. "You don't mean every pencil?"

"Of course, every pencil!"

We cranked up some festive tunes on the stereo and got to work. Even with the mass-production assembly line we set up, it still took a couple of wonderful hours. We made it to the theater just in time for the ten o'clock showing. All the laughter and camaraderie throughout the evening made the movie all the more enjoyable. Sandra Bullock had never been so funny.

Debbie never did fit all the goodies into her family's stockings—some ended up under the tree, as happened almost every year.

It was a great lesson for me to put Michael's stocking obsession into perspective. Compared to the rest of the family, he's tame.

We've come to a happy compromise on our Christmas stockings: each year, we agree on a spending limit. This limit changes every year, depending on our circumstances, but at least now we're in line with each other. The tangerine thing is still a stumper at times, though. Since Michael does most of the fruit shopping, I tend to stick to the basics. If it's small, round, and orange, it must be a tangerine. Right?

Even if it's not small, round, or orange.

One year, Michael's tangerine was an apple, but it was in the toe, so that should count for something. Right? A rose by any other name...

Traditions are great. They add meaning to our lives, help us understand how we fit in, and give us something to look forward to. Traditions are comforting, letting us know what to expect.

But they should *add* to the celebration, not make us prisoners of it.

"The Year of the Apple" was a great reminder of this. We were out of tangerines, and I knew the grocery store would be a madhouse on Christmas Eve. Rather than stress out by setting foot in that bedlam, I modified the tradition that year.

When circumstances change, we have the choice of maintaining old traditions or creating new ones. Getting married, having children move out of the home, finding oneself alone at Christmas due to death, divorce, or job relocation—all these circumstances may call for modified traditions. There are still traditions you can keep or create.

Our single friend David from the choir joined an old-fashioned caroling group a few years ago that looks like something from a Dickens novel. David, who has a gorgeous baritone-bass voice, enjoys singing in four-part harmony, clad in his Victorian finery, at various holiday events around town. (*And* he gets paid for it in the process!) Win-win.

Our old friends Curt and Peggy incorporated a tradition into their family that began in Curt's family when he was small.

"After Christmas, when all the decorations were being put away," Peggy related, "little Curt would write a note to himself and stick it in his stocking so he could read it the following year when the stockings were unpacked. We began having our boys, Ryan and Don, do that when they were young as well. Their note might include hobbies they were interested in at the time, things going on at school, a little picture they drew, or plans for the coming year. Curt and I joined in this, too. It's fun to read and share these things the following year when the Christmas things are brought out."

Michael's former boss, Kendra, also has a great "paper" tradition. She and her husband both have trinket-box ornaments hanging on their tree. Every year, they fold up a little something and put it inside the respective trinket box ornament. It could be movie passes, a gift certificate, concert tickets, or any number of things. This is the last gift they open.

"And every year I forget about the ornaments," Kendra said. "We unwrap all the presents under the tree, and I think we're done. Derek has to remind me there's one gift left, and then it's like an added bonus."

"A Christmas encore," Michael called it, the performer that he is.

When Michael was still single and working at a theater company in Texas, November and December were the company's busiest months of the year. Those two months were also the same season when all the good movies opened. The actors didn't have time to see any of the films though—they were onstage performing themselves. The theater troupe didn't work on Christmas Eve or Christmas Day, though, so those two days became their movie marathons. Most of the company didn't have family in the area—except for each other—so it worked out well. Michael said that one year he saw two movies on December 24 and *three* on the 25th.

That was a tradition.

Moving back to California, my husband tried to keep a bit of that tradition alive. He and I even managed to squeeze in a movie on Christmas Day the first year of our marriage. But with family from both sides in town, it became too difficult to fit in a movie every Christmas. We did it a few times, but we had to be discreet.

Every family has a secret language or special code words that mean something only to them. Michael and I decided that "nap" is code for matinee. On Christmas Day, we'd tell family we were tired and really needed a nap, but would be back in time for Christmas dinner. We managed to keep our "naps" secret for a few years, but eventually someone in the family figured it out—my nephew, or one of Michael's nieces, I can't remember which.

Busted.

Ever since then, other family members have been joining us for our annual Christmas Day "nap."

The most fun was the year *Mamma Mia* was released. I'm a huge Abba fan, having been stationed in Europe in the '70s when disco was big and doing my "Dancing Queen" thing on the dance floor every weekend. Now, all those years later, Abba had become popular once again, and their music was on the big screen—sung by Meryl Streep, no less! I'd been itching to see this musical onscreen for months ever since I read about it during its filming. That Christmas, we made it a "girls' day out" with my two nieces and my sister-in-law accompanying us. (Michael was virtually the only guy in the theater.)

We had a blast. Such a joyous, exuberant film. We tapped our feet, swayed to the music, and had huge smiles on our faces throughout the entire movie. (I dare anyone not to tap their feet when they hear "Dancing Queen.") That movie has a permanent place in our DVD collection (yes, we still watch DVDs; we're old.) Anytime I'm feeling down or discouraged about the state of the world or a difficult situation in my life, I pop in *Mamma Mia*—either the original or the sequel, featuring Cher—to put a smile on my face. (The moment Cher sings "Fernando" is sublime. Or, as Tom Hanks says, "Perfection." Don't believe me? Google Tom Hanks, Cher, and Fernando on *The Graham Norton Show*.)

But back to traditions. I always enjoy hearing about other people's Christmas traditions.

My eighty-one-year-old friend Sandy said the family tradition that sticks with her from childhood is of her dad receiving thick construction socks every Christmas, with white toes and red heels—"the kind people used to make sock monkeys out of," she said. (The red heels made the monkey's lips.)

"For our Christmas stockings, my mother filled Dad's sturdy new socks with oranges, apples, candy, and nuts for us three girls," Sandy recounted to me. "As a result, the socks would stretch. The more things she put in, the longer they stretched. She'd have to wash them before giving them to Dad as his gift, so they stretched back into shape." Sandy also recalled her mother telling her that if she didn't leave out a stick of butter for *Pai Natal* (the Portuguese Santa Claus), he would bite off one of her toes.

My mom told us that if *we* were bad, Santa would put coal in our stockings. Now *that* I could handle. (Although I never had to since I was always so well-behaved. Just call me Goody Two-Shoes.)

Tradition Tips

Throughout this book, I have been sharing, and will continue to share, many of our holiday traditions with you. Goodness knows, we have plenty of them. We try not to get so locked into the traditions, though, that we forget to have fun. If your tradition only adds stress and no joy, can you live without it for a year?

For instance, we usually put up three or four Christmas trees in various rooms of the house and go all out on decorating for the holiday. This year, however, we were both especially busy with work projects and other commitments that consumed much of our time. The idea of putting up four trees and having to trim them, not to mention pulling out bin after bin of all the other decorations we usually display, made me twitch.

We agreed to skip the trees, Michael's Father Christmas collection, and most of the myriad decorations. We kept it simple instead, with greenery on the mantel, a fresh evergreen wreath on the door, Michael's jewel tree "forest" atop the buffet, a poinsettia, my lovely Christmas china on the dining room table, and several candles.*

Just right.

*Oops, I forgot. Mr. Christmas couldn't stand the idea of no tree at all, so while I was writing furiously to meet a deadline, he decorated the four-foot-tall metal Eiffel Tower that stands in the dining room, aka "the travel tree."

8

Christmas Without Children

Christmas waves a magic wand over this world, and behold, everything is softer and more beautiful.
—Norman Vincent Peale

Baking Christmas cookies, wrapping presents to put beneath the tree, watching *Rudolph the Red-Nosed Reindeer* for the zillionth time with the kids…wait a minute. What if there aren't any kids? What's Christmas like without children?

Just as special, but in different ways.

Christmas is a time for families, and a husband and wife make up their own family. Often, though, couples without children tend to get overlooked on this seemingly tailor-made-for-kids holiday.

Many couples don't have children. Some make the choice, others have the choice made for them; some are still newlyweds; some have already "been there, done that," and their children have flown the nest to distant climes and are now feathering their own nests. Whatever the circumstances, not having kids shouldn't diminish the childlike joy we experience at Christmas.

Besides, who's to say *we* can't be the children in our Christmas story? Michael often says, "It's never too late to have a happy childhood."

That happy childhood is never more evident in our own home than at Christmastime, when we deck the halls, make fudge and popcorn balls, and set up the train under the tree.

Charles Dickens, in his iconic work *A Christmas Carol*, said, "It is good to be children sometimes, and never better than at Christmas, when its mighty Founder was a child Himself."

Amen to that.

In the Walker family of four—including the latest additions, our rescue dogs Peanut and Poppy, go all-out for our favorite holiday. We shop year-round, keeping our eyes peeled in bookstores and one-of-a-kind boutiques for just the right present for each person on our list. Michael starts as early as February or March making special handcrafted gifts for the upcoming holiday. We've even been known to host a "Christmas in July" party when we get a hankering for the winter festivities during the heat of a California summer.

Michael and I were individual Christmas nuts before we met, but together, we're a whole pile of chestnuts roasting on an open fire. Although we don't have kids, we don't let that stop us from celebrating this most special of days that began with the most important birth in history.

Celebrating the birth of a baby when you can't have your own, though, can be difficult.

After years of infertility treatments and disappointments, my friend Laurie simply couldn't face another Christmas with step-grandchildren and extended family.

"I wanted to escape, to find a place where there were no children at Christmas," Laurie recalled. "Although it seemed shocking and selfish at the time, my husband and I decided to bow out of all the holiday hoopla and head to Maui for two weeks instead. Some family members were sure we'd be totally homesick and regret it. Nothing remotely like that happened. Instead, we were freed from the overspending and last-minute gift buying. Freed from the endless crowds and advertisements. Freed from making my home like something Martha [Stewart] would approve of. Freed from a hot stove in the kitchen and then cleaning up.

"Instead," Laurie went on, "I learned to surf and indulged myself in my new sport every morning. We explored the island, went snorkeling, and ate delicious meals under swaying palm trees. We saw the green flash at sunset. (If the weather is right—clear and humid—the moment the sun dips below the horizon, an unexplained bright green flash occurs.) We went to a casual outdoor Christmas Eve service where everyone wore leis and sang under the stars. It was relaxing, romantic, and more fun than we could have imagined.

"Sometimes you need to just get away to bolster yourself and your marriage," she concluded.

True. And one of these years, Michael and I are planning to do just that. (England at Christmastime tops our list.) We're waiting for Santa to stick a couple of airline tickets in our stockings. Meanwhile, we'll continue to enjoy our California Christmases with friends and relatives.

My former air force roommate, Diane, and her husband, Warren, always spent Christmas alone together since their respective families lived in other states. Two weeks before the holiday, with a pot of potpourri simmering on the stove and sending its fragrance throughout the house and Christmas music playing, they'd put up their tree. "All the memories of Germany and England come back when I put the ornaments we got over there on the tree," Diane recalled.

The couple also enjoyed cooking Christmas dinner together—food, and its preparation played a big role in their household.

"We usually don't buy huge gifts for each other, but a lot of little gifts instead," Diane told me. "I'm happy getting Earl Grey tea, honey mustard pretzels, Red Vines, and Sour Patch Kids. Just a few of my favorite things, and you can eat every gift! I love to eat—it's my favorite pastime in life. I guess I've always believed, 'If I can't eat it or wear it, I don't need it.' Warren gets off pretty easily shopping for me at the grocery store," she related with a twinkle in her eye.

Kyle and Lesley, some other friends of ours, begin their Christmas season in early December with their church's musical extravaganza.

"Excitement builds at the steps of the main entrance of the auditorium with a mandatory hug with Father Christmas," English-born Lesley related. "Then, into the show—an hour and a half of singing, clapping, laughing, and, occasionally, a tear.

"The next day welcomes in the seasonal trauma of untwisting the lights and checking the strings for duff [bad] bulbs," she shared. "It's Kyle's job to hang the lights, and I busy myself with the dressing of the tree. When the main lights are dimmed and the candles lit, it's all a little reminiscent of the disco era as the flickering light dances its way across all the sparkly hanging ornaments."

Christmas Eve kicks off Kyle and Lesley's traditional Christmas movie marathon. They turn off their phones and "shut down the hatches" so they won't be disturbed as they snuggle in with their holiday favorites on the small screen. On Christmas morning, they exchange gifts, Lesley makes Kyle his favorite pancakes, and she calls her family in England. Then it's back to their movie marathon, followed by lunch at one of Kyle's sisters' houses, where the whole family gathers to celebrate and exchange gifts.

Christmas night is theirs, though, Lesley stressed: "Me, hubby, and the pooch."

Then, there are our friends Ryan and Ella, who didn't get together until they were in their late thirties. Ella recounted to me that Ryan hadn't enjoyed Christmas all that much growing up because, in his household, everything to do with the holiday was so regimented and had to be done a certain way. As someone who'd been single a long time, Ryan would do one or two things with his buddies over the holidays, but not much.

When they married, the couple had discussions about how they wanted to observe Christmas as a couple, to redeem some of those holiday celebrations that hadn't been bright spots in childhood. Before she met Ryan, Ella had been celebrating Advent—the four-week season on the liturgical church calendar anticipating the arrival of Jesus—for years. Now, the two of them do so together, lighting the candle every week and doing a devotional reading. Ella also gets them both Advent calendars for adults with fun little surprises behind each Advent door. She calls this "a little extra joy boost."

Each year, the couple has a Christmas meeting in advance of the season where they ask one another, "What would be the top three things we can do this season that would feel like Christmas to you, but not be tiring or overwhelming?" Ella recounted. "It's slightly different every year, depending on work and energy levels."

One of the things they always try to do is observe Saint Nicholas Day on December 6. "That's the day we make all our charitable donations for the year," Ella said. "We focus on organizations that help women, preferring to donate to women's and children's causes."

Saint Nicholas of Myra is said to have rescued three girls from being forced into prostitution by dropping a sack of gold coins in their house to cover their dowries. In honor of his Turkish roots,

Ryan and Ella have a Mediterranean feast for Christmas dinner. "One year," Ella recalled, "we had a cocktail party where we had everyone come over and make a donation."

Saint Nicholas would have been pleased.

Ryan and Ella are big J. R. R. Tolkien fans, so they celebrate Tolkien's birthday, on December 3. They'll eat something "Englishy, like shepherd's pie," Ella said, and either read Tolkien aloud together or watch *The Lord of the Rings* trilogy. And since Saint Lucy's Day is December 13, often they'll go get their Christmas tree on that day.

I'd never heard of Saint Lucy's Day before Ella mentioned it, so I asked her to explain its significance to me.

It's a feast day honoring Saint Lucia from Italy, who brought food to fourth-century Christians escaping persecution by hiding in the Roman catacombs. Lucia wore candles in a wreath on her head to light her way in the darkness and to keep her hands free for distributing food. Every year on Saint Lucy's Day, Italian Christians do a procession in what is known as a "festival of light" with girls in white dresses wearing crowns of candles.

Saint Lucy's Day is not confined to Italy or Italian communities, though. It's also a big celebration in Sweden and other Scandinavian countries because it symbolizes the return of light during the long, dark winter months. Being Swedish, Ella grew up with this tradition. "For the home celebration, the eldest daughter gets up before everyone else and makes Santa Lucia buns—special saffron buns—and serves them to her family," she told me. "We don't have a daughter to do that, so we do our own version by getting donuts or cinnamon buns."

Another holiday tradition of Ryan and Ella's is driving around looking at Christmas lights while they listen to favorite Christmas music from childhood. "We bring hot chocolate and listen to cheesy music as we look at the lights," Ella said.

The couple also has a list of Christmas movies they try to watch together each year, including *Elf*, *A Charlie Brown Christmas*, *A Christmas Story*, *While You Were Sleeping*, and a Finnish film I'd never heard of before called *Rare Exports*.

"The movie's in Finnish, and very Scandinavian—Finnish sensibilities are very different than American," Ella explained, adding that the fairy tale depicted in the film, rooted in Northern European legend and lore, isn't for everyone—particularly impressionable children. (One reviewer said the movie's St. Nick is informed more by the Brothers Grimm than Norman Rockwell.) Ella likes it, though, because there's an adorable Scandinavian child who winds up saving Christmas for everyone.

"None of what we do at Christmas is rigid," Ella told me. "If we miss something, that's all right."

One of the things she and Ryan enjoy is having *A Christmas Story* playing in the background on Christmas Day while they're making food. This tradition is a carryover from when Ella was growing up and one of the cable channels used to play the movie on repeat, so it was always on in the background.

"We tend to do a lot of hooking different traditions together," Ella said. "We have a special meal on this day, watch a special show on this day, listen to specific music on this day. We don't do a ton of gifts, but we always make sure we do stockings." Growing up, their respective households had different traditions, so the couple decided to establish their own: exchanging presents on Christmas Eve and opening their stockings on Christmas morning. "We'll do appetizers on Christmas Eve and open presents in between church services," she recounted. "Christmas morning, I make cinnamon rolls, and we open our stockings while we play Bing Crosby's Christmas album."

The couple also plays board games. "I usually get us a new game on Christmas," Ella said. "We open that on Christmas Eve and play it on Christmas Day." Last year, she bought Qwirkle, a mix-and-match strategy game where players create lines of tiles that are all one color or all one shape.

Ryan and Ella spread out their family celebrations so they're not doing them all at once. For instance, they'll have tea with Ryan's sister one day and dinner with their parents another day.

They celebrate all twelve days of Christmas and, on Twelfth Night—January 6—make breakfast for dinner and invite people over to play games. "It's the last hurrah of the season," Ella said. Having bought a loaf of panettone sometime during the season, they'll use that for French toast for their Twelfth Night breakfast dinner, accompanied by sparkling cider or "something with bubbles."

Thanks for all these great tradition ideas, Ella! I think Michael and I are going to incorporate some of them next year.

For couples having trouble carving out time alone together, just the two of you, on Christmas Day, my English friend Patricia from Dorset has a surefire solution. "No more Christmases at our house as the place everyone comes for lunch. Tell them you are a vegetarian. It works like a charm, especially if you throw in words like 'tofu' and 'Quorn.'"

Patricia thinks a vegetarian Christmas is much more interesting than the same old, same old, served in most households. "Last year," she told me, "our Christmas was a Mexican theme, while our neighbors had a Caribbean Christmas. We found them sitting out in the conservatory in their most colorful shorts and T-shirts with the table covered in a whole range of exotic fruits and vegetables," Patricia said. "Strangely enough, they don't get any unwanted visitors."

She has a point. I confess, however, that I don't think I could go without my traditional turkey or ham on Christmas Day. Besides, I can't even say "Quorn," much less know what it is.

Twosome Tip

Make sure you carve out some special "alone" time together as a couple during the holidays—even if you have kids. Ask a friend or family member to babysit so you can enjoy a movie, dinner, a long walk, or even some last-minute shopping. It's important to connect with each other during the craziness of the season, to focus just on the two of you.

9

Taking the Bah Out of Humbug

If I could work my will,...every idiot who goes about with "Merry Christmas" on his lips, should be boiled with his own pudding, and buried with a stake of holly through his heart.
—Ebenezer Scrooge

Bah humbug.

Too commercial. Too expensive. Too exhausting.

"Tom" was a grown-up who didn't like Christmas—the Scrooge to end all Scrooges.

Until he met Lily.

He admits that, growing up, Christmas didn't like him, so the feeling became mutual. As the youngest of seven kids, Tom always got hand-me-downs. His parents, who struggled to make ends meet, got one kind of socks for their sons: solid white and interchangeable. Just wash, dry, grab any two, and stuff them in a drawer. Any boy's drawer, since they were all fished from the same sock pool.

Tom ached for colored socks so he could be like the rest of the kids at school. One year, that's all he asked for at Christmas. His parents bought him several pairs—all mustard yellow.

Tom said he felt humiliated. Sure, in the grand scheme of things, socks may not seem all that important. After all, he had food to eat and a place to call home. He had clothing too, including shoes and socks.

Christmas isn't about physical needs, though; it's emotional and spiritual, and this little boy's spirit was being chipped away.

This is the same kid who participated in a white elephant gift exchange when he was in Boy Scouts. His take-home gift was a prune.

These are just two of the many disappointments Tom experienced during his formative years. In order to get through the holidays, he stopped caring.

Michael and I have a theory that many people are Scrooges because of disappointment. But it doesn't have to stay that way.

Tom met Lily. Lily loved Christmas, but every significant romantic relationship of hers had ended with the man bailing out just before the holidays.

When Tom married Lily, they decided to redeem Christmas for one another.

According to the *Merriam-Webster Dictionary*, redeem means "to buy back, to free from what distresses or harms, or to change for the better, repair, restore." When Tom and Lily got married, they started new holiday traditions, and now, several years later, Christmas is a wonderful time for them both.

Tom, in particular, has learned how to have fun with the season. It's called planning. One year, he restored an old, illuminated clock that had been in Lily's dad's barn for decades, since before his wife could remember. Now the clock sits on Lily and Tom's entertainment center. Tom had the clockworks professionally rebuilt, but he rewired the lights himself. For the man who describes himself as "technologically challenged," this was no small feat. Tom taught himself as he went along.

This huge act of love makes the clock all the more precious to Lily.

Taking the time to plan and then spending the energy to execute that plan does much to make the season bright.

Although much of her season is bright, our friend Rebecca is a little "Scrooged-off" about Christmas cards.

Rebecca wants to know why, when she got married, she had to assume the job of writing all her spouse's Christmas cards. "I love my husband to death, and he's generally a wonderful, enlightened man," she said, "but I was really surprised the first Christmas after we got married when he started rolling off a list of his friends and relatives that I needed to send cards to. Of course, he only started mentioning it a week before December 25."

His reasoning? She's the writer in the family.

He'll sign the cards—bulk-production style—to help, but it's Rebecca's job to keep up with any address changes and to write all the messages. "To this day, I write all the Christmas cards, and struggle with finding clever little things to say to relatives of his I've never met, and to pretend those notes are heartfelt and from both of us," she told me. "All this to relatives and obscure friends he never ever contacts (except for my 'Merry Christmas' cards each year!)."

If I was Rebecca, I'd go on strike.

Other men we know can't stand shopping. Our former neighbor, Al, for example, never purchased gifts for his wife, Dolores, but instead gave her money to go pick out something she wanted.

Another girlfriend of mine—quite the fashionista—does her own Christmas shopping too, since shopping isn't her husband's thing, either. She'll spend a day in her favorite shops and return home with new outfits, shoes, and a designer purse, informing her husband of the Christmas presents he got her.

My uncle Jimmy also hates shopping, preferring to never set foot in a store. Instead, every year he clips envelopes filled with money for his wife and kids to the Christmas tree. He does it for the grandkids now, too.

Some people are just natural-born Scrooges.

The solution? Celebrate around them. Eventually, they may join in the Christmas cheer, especially if you tease them enough. Or maybe not. Some people just like being the Grinch.

Hmm. None of these men has a dog. Maybe, just maybe, if they had a dog named Max, they could put little antlers on his ears and…but that's another story.

Being a Scrooge isn't confined to men—women can be Scrooges too. Although "Scroogeywoman" doesn't have quite the same ring to it as "Scroogeyman." (See below.)

Grumpy Scroogeymen Advice

(Michael and I coined the term Scroogeymen years ago.)

If you have a grumpy Scroogeyman (or woman) in your life, try singing this song we wrote (to the tune of "God Rest Ye Merry, Gentlemen"). Maybe they'll change their tune.

God rest ye, grumpy Scroogeymen, let no one you dismay.
Remember joy at Christmastime, at least on Christmas Day.
Don't be a jerk, take off from work, let Rudolph light your way.
And find kids to play with today, hear what I say.
And don't forget to be a kid today!

10

You'll Go Down in His Story

(FINDING THE MEANING BEHIND WELL-KNOWN ICONS AT CHRISTMAS.)

> *History is only a confused heap of facts.*
> —Earl of Chesterfield

Michael and I are trivia buffs—it's one of the things that drew us together in our dating days.

My husband's fascination with useless tidbits of information is so strong that, back in the day, he had a lunch-hour appointment every Wednesday to play Trivial Pursuit with his work buddies Jerry and Jean. Over time, these weekly sessions spilled over into the occasional weekend game of Trivial Pursuit at our house or the home of Jerry and Jean, Michael's work friends. Fun times. My best two categories are pink and brown: entertainment and literature.

I've had a love affair with movies since childhood, when my dad would let my sister and me stay up late to watch old movies with him. *Old* being a relative term—I'm talking classics from the '30s, '40s, and '50s: Bogie and Bacall, Rogers and Astaire, Tracy and Hepburn, Bette Davis, Jimmy Stewart, Ingrid Bergman, Gene Kelly, Judy Garland, the delicious Cary Grant, and a host of others—which is why I prefer Silver Screen Trivial Pursuit. I'm very competitive, though, bordering on obnoxious, although I've mellowed in recent years. My dogged competitiveness is why I'm only "allowed" to play the Silver Screen edition once a year—on my birthday—with friends. (Not to brag, but, on a few occasions, it was Laura versus the room.)

So, the merging of trivia and Christmas was a natural combination for the two of us. Although we've both acquired lots of information over the years, it wasn't until preparing this chapter that I—with Michael's help—did any significant research.

Michael is especially fond of Christmas music trivia. For instance, did you know that "The Christmas Song" was written during a heat wave in July? The story goes that two songwriters were collaborating to create music for a film. Because of the heat, lyricist Robert Wells was trying to cool down by making a list of "winter" things. Then Mel Tormé noticed the lists, and in just forty minutes, a song was born. "Chestnuts roasting on an open fire...."

Another Hollywood trivia tidbit is that the song "White Christmas" is not originally from the film of the same name. More than a decade earlier, Irving Berlin had written the song for a Bing Crosby/Fred Astaire movie musical called *Holiday Inn*. Rumor has it the songwriter didn't care for the song initially, until Bing convinced him to keep it in the show. It won the Oscar for Best Song in 1942 and is now the bestselling Christmas song of all time.

I'll bet you didn't know that "Jingle Bells" was really written for Thanksgiving, did you? Commissioned for a Thanksgiving church service in Medford, Massachusetts, the song was so well-received that the choir did an encore for the Christmas service. Going forward, "Jingle Bells" became associated with the Christmas holiday.

A few years ago, Michael became involved with an online music trivia game, competing against many thousands of people from all over the world. Games were a one-on-one competition with whoever happened to be online at the time in any one of dozens of categories. Rankings were by region, day, month, and overall. One of Michael's favorite categories was Christmas music. He was usually in the top ten for California and once managed to reach the first-place slot worldwide.

Yes, he spent many hours on this game.

There's lots of information out there about Christmas, some of it trivial, but it seems like the history of the holiday and its traditions take on more weight because it is, after all, His story.

Have you ever stopped to think why we hack down trees and bring them inside our homes just for them to dry out and drop needles all over the place? Why we hang stockings by the fire when we have clothes dryers? Or kiss somebody just because they're standing under the mistletoe? It's a parasitic plant!

Then there's the big guy in the red suit, who probably has more aliases than anybody found on the FBI's Ten Most Wanted Fugitives list.

Does all of this relate somehow to the baby in the manger?

Sure. Most of it, anyway. Just to warn you, though, some of our beliefs are not quite historical truths. Take Jesus's birthday, for example.

Historians agree that December 25 is *not* the exact date Jesus was born. Most likely, His birthday would have been in the springtime, when shepherds would have been *"living out in the fields nearby, keeping watch over their flocks at night"* (Luke 2:8).

It wasn't until the fourth century that December 25 was officially declared the Feast of the Nativity. Although the birth of Jesus was celebrated by Christians on different days in various places around the world, this unified most everyone to the same day, shifting the focus away from pagan revelry.

For centuries, the winter solstice has been a time of great celebration for many cultures worldwide. Occurring on December 22 or 23, depending on the year, it's the shortest day and longest night of the year. In Roman times, Saturnalia was a major festival dedicated to the Roman god Saturn, held during the winter solstice. Since people were going to celebrate anyway, church leaders picked that time for their sacred holiday.

Similarly, many churches today host harvest festivals or "Trunk or Treat" on October 31 as an alternative to the pagan Halloween activities.

Criticism that Christmas has strayed from the pure and "true meaning" has been around from the beginning. From the early days, it was said there was too much of the old Saturnalia traditions blended into the Feast of the Nativity. And so it went through the centuries as different people blended their cultural and Christian traditions together.

In the sixteenth century, the Puritans in England even set about to outlaw all festivals, including Christmas. They succeeded during the era of the Commonwealth—the mid-1600s, or the period when Parliament was established and ruled in place of the kings and queens.

Pilgrims brought this same zeal against Christmas to America. In fact, it was illegal to celebrate Christmas in parts of New England until shortly before the Civil War. Many ignored these laws, however. Although people were unable to hold public celebrations, they continued to enjoy the holiday in the privacy of their homes.

As people from different cultures moved to the New World, they brought with them their traditions. America, being a melting pot, incorporated these traditions, and Christmas evolved.

Disclaimer: I'm not giving you a thorough history of Christmas in this chapter, simply hitting highlights of the things I found interesting. There's a plethora of information available in books and online. Try typing "history of Christmas" into any search engine.

Having said that, here are the histories of some of our holiday icons. (Apologies in advance to those whose customs and traditions I've omitted.)

The Christmas tree originated in Germany—the triangular fir tree was meant to symbolize the Holy Trinity—and Protestant reformer Martin Luther is credited with first putting candles on trees in the sixteenth century.

Trees were popularized in England by Prince Albert and Queen Victoria. Albert, being German, brought trees into Windsor Castle for the Royal Family to enjoy. (An engraving of the time showed the queen, the prince, and their children decorating a tree, igniting the public's interest in doing so as well.)

Christmas carols date back centuries, but Saint Francis of Assisi first incorporated them into church services in the thirteenth century. Until then, the hymns used in services were somber songs usually sung in Latin. Lively folk songs were enjoyed by the public in other settings but not in church.

Saint Francis was also the one who popularized the crèche, or nativity scene. Christmas—and animal—lover that he was, he had a live Bethlehem scene reenacted for his followers to explain the birth of Jesus. The nativity caught on, both in the form of the live scene and the miniature figures, which have been enjoyed ever since.

In America today, our nativity scenes usually consist of a dozen or so figures, but some cultures' scenes depict in the entire town of Bethlehem. Some scenes include hundreds of figures! Not to mention all the buildings and other scenery.

Hmm. Sounds familiar. Reminds me of the popular Christmas villages people like to collect.

But back to Christmas carols.... The favorite carol story in our house is the tale of "O Holy Night." I've loved that song since I sang it in the cherub choir at church with my sister when I was four. (Michael, on the other hand, has loved it ever since he heard it played as a piano solo by his second-grade teacher.) We both think it's the most beautiful carol ever written.

In 1847, a French poet named Placide Cappeau was asked by the local parish priest to write a Christmas poem. A few years later, the poet's friend Adolphe Adam, a Parisian composer known for writing the classical ballet *Giselle*, wrote music to accompany the lyrics of the poem; thus, "Cantique de Noël" was born.

"Cantique de Noël" became popular among the French and was sung in many Christmas services. In time though, Placide Cappeau left the French Catholic Church to become part of the Socialist movement, and rumors that composer Adolphe Adam was Jewish began circulating. The Catholic Church in France condemned the song because it was written by an alleged Jew and a Socialist.

A decade later, John Sullivan Dwight, an American minister, writer, and fervent abolitionist, translated the song into English and was moved by the lines, "Chains shall he break, for the slave is our brother, and in his name, all oppression shall cease." When this American minister published his translation of "O Holy Night," the song became a favorite in the US, particularly the Northern states, during the Civil War.

This beloved carol has other historical significance as well: it was the first song played on the radio. On Christmas Eve, 1906, the first-ever broadcast, the Christmas story from the Gospel of Luke was read over the air, followed by "O Holy Night" played on a violin.

Other carol stories are a mix of fact and fiction.

The story behind "Silent Night" is fairly common knowledge. The organ broke in a small Austrian town's church one Christmas Eve, so the frantic priest brought the local schoolteacher a poem he'd written and asked him to set it to music. Hours later, to guitar accompaniment rather than organ, "Silent Night" made its debut. What is not common knowledge is that the poem was written two days earlier rather than on the day of the service.

"God Rest Ye Merry, Gentlemen" takes on a different meaning when you consider the evolution of the English language and some missing punctuation. Most people don't realize there is a comma in the title. Though we sing the original words, their meaning has changed over the years. A proper translation in today's language would be something like "God make you mighty, gentlemen."

Remember that the next time you wish someone a *"Merry Christmas."*

Then there's "The Twelve Days of Christmas," probably the biggest Internet urban legend of our time. If you have email or are on Facebook, you've undoubtedly read that this song was a secret catechism of Catholics in England during the 1500s. The story goes that the song was a memory aid during an era when it might have been too dangerous to write things down.

A cool story, but it's not true. The story only goes back to 1995, when an article about the secret catechism was published, then later withdrawn. The earliest records of the song being sung come from the eighteenth century, not the sixteenth.

Personally, Michael likes the myth and the intrigue. And it *has* helped him remember the words to the song: Jesus had twelve disciples, or apostles, so those are the drummers drumming (there are also twelve distinct points in the Apostles' Creed); there were eleven faithful apostles; they're the pipers piping.

Not having grown up in a "high church" where Advent was observed, I also learned the twelve days of Christmas are not the days leading up to December 25. Christmas is actually Day One, leading up to Day Six, known as the Epiphany, when it's believed the magi arrived to visit the Christ child. Some denominations in Western Christianity may know the magi as Caspar, Melchior, and Balthazar, but, historically, we don't even know if there were three of them. It was interpreted that there were three men because of the gifts—gold, frankincense, and myrrh—but the Bible only says there were wise men from the East. (See Matthew 2:1.)

It could have been three, could have been dozens.

Other traditions tie mistletoe to Christmas. A solstice accompaniment in pre-Christian England, the church replaced it with holly and ivy as evergreen decorations. Mistletoe was popular in Victorian times and remains associated with the season.

Which brings us to Santa Claus.

Today's Santa is an amalgam, like much of American culture. As people immigrated to the United States, they brought along their culture's holiday traditions, many of which included a supernatural gift-giver. Though often male, sometimes the gift giver is female, like Italy's *La Befana*, the repentant witch who misdirected the magi. Now, she gives gifts to all children in atonement for delaying the wise men's search for the Christ child.

Other female gift-givers are Russia's *Babushka*, a grandmotherly old lady, and the German *Kriskind*, an angelic, fair-haired girl who wears the crown of candles. From this, we get the name Kris Kringle. In Spain and many Latin American cultures, it's the wise men themselves who bring gifts.

In England, Santa is known as Father Christmas; in France, *Père Noël*; but the gift-giver we know today in the US has as his basis a bishop who lived from around AD 280–350 in Asia Minor—present-day Turkey. Imprisoned for his faith by Emperor Diocletian, he was released several years later when the Christian Emperor Constantine the Great came to power.

Nicholas, Bishop of Myra, became Saint Nicholas, patron saint of children. In one of the most famous stories about him, a poor man was going to have to sell his three daughters into slavery because he had no dowry to offer for them. On three separate occasions, a bag of money arrived at their home from an anonymous donor during the night, one for each of the girls, so that they could afford to get married. (One version of the story has the money bag being thrown down the chimney and landing in a stocking—this is partly where the tradition of Christmas stockings began.) Nicholas, of course, brought the gifts.

Throughout the centuries, Saint Nicholas has remained the favorite in Holland. His name in Dutch is *Sinterklass*, which evolved into our Santa Claus.

Much of the personality of America's Santa comes from the 1822 poem by Clement Moore, "A Visit from St. Nicholas," known these days by its first line: "'Twas the night before Christmas…"

A few decades later, Thomas Nast, a political cartoonist, published his drawings of Moore's version of Santa Claus. It was a Depression-era advertising campaign, however, that gave us the image of Santa we know and love today. The company was Coca-Cola. Ever notice how Santa's suit and the Coke label are the same shade of red? Intentional. (I wonder if the people who say Christmas has become too commercial are aware that our modern-day Santa was created to push a product. It does lend a certain credibility to the argument.)

Which leads us to Rudolph.

The red-nosed reindeer was originally a marketing gimmick as well, created in 1939 for Montgomery Ward department stores. Commissioned as a booklet to be given away to shoppers, the story was based in part on the tale of the ugly duckling and has grown to become a staple in our Christmas treasury.

The traditions of Christmas are many and rich. I hope you've gained more from this chapter than just tidbits of knowledge to be used in Trivial Pursuit. (Although that's not a bad thing.)

Some traditions are spiritual in nature, some humanitarian, and some economic. If they add to your celebration, so much the better. Merry Christmas!

Historical Tips

This year, consider sharing with others the history of the icons of Christmas. I've told you about some of them here, but what other icons do you include in your holiday celebration? Maybe do a little research of your own and explore their origins by asking such questions as...

Why do we eat turkey at Christmas?

What exactly is the story behind the Advent candle?

Why are billions of Christmas cards mailed each year?

Knowing the whys might help you enjoy them all the more.

11

That's the Woman Who Rocks

(CHRISTMAS PARTY IDEAS AND FUN WAYS TO AVOID COMMON PARTY PITFALLS)

> *We do not remember days, we remember moments.*
> —Cesare Pavese

I've never been a big party girl—especially when it comes to parties with lots of people and loud noise. I prefer my parties to be smaller and more intimate. If there's a game involved, all the better.

Michael and I have perfected some great party games over the years. One of our favorites is the white elephant gift exchange at Christmas. However, that phrase is not the best nomenclature Historically, the term came from Asia, where such a gift was actually a burden rather than a blessing. Since white elephants were sacred, they could never be put to work. Whoever received a white elephant was then obligated to feed and care for the animal throughout its extremely long lifetime (elephants live about as long as humans). Quite a financial drain.

Many of you are familiar with the white elephant gift exchange game: everyone brings a wrapped gift, you all draw numbers, and, when your number comes up, you can either open a new gift or steal something someone has already unwrapped. If your gift is stolen, you get to choose a new gift or steal someone else's. It's fun when done the traditional way, but we think it's even better with our modifications.

So as not to cause additional financial stress during the holidays, we prefer white elephant gifts to be garage sale-type items—not anything you have to buy, but rather, something you have around the house you don't want anymore. We tell people it's more fun if they bring something someone might actually want to steal.

One year, Michael opened papier-mâché fruit. It was obvious no one would want to steal that, so he sat back and watched, knowing the game was over for him. I previously mentioned our friend Tom's receiving a prune at a Boy Scouts white elephant exchange. Even worse than that was the year someone brought a half-eaten hamburger to our friends' white elephant event. Yes, this really happened. I was there.

On the other end of the spectrum, one year at another friend's white elephant event, there were several gifts worth stealing—in particular, a beautiful, handcrafted eight-by-ten-inch framed paper cutting of the nativity. The game got exciting as that gift bounced from person to person, with everyone stealing it. The problem was that the present kept bouncing, and it seemed as if the game would never end. The next year, we added the rule that every gift could only be stolen three times—whoever got it on the third steal wound up with the present.

Back in the day, we'd go to a white elephant gift exchange hosted by Michael's quilting mentor, Nela, and her husband, Chuck. Nela and Chuck don't have a Christmas party every year, but when they do, it's a lot of fun and a nice reunion of my husband's old quilting pals. One year, one of the women at the party opened a gift that made her blush: a black lace teddy. And not just any teddy either—an over-the-top, tacky, Frederick's of Hollywood teddy. Embarrassed, she urged others to steal it.

The following year, the tacky teddy was back, and one of the husbands opened it. The year after that, it reappeared stuffed in a jelly jar. Everyone had suspected it was in one of the packages, but no one expected it to be in *that* package. Homemade preserves, yes; teddy, no.

The white elephant game is great for a group of ten or more people. We've played it with more than twenty, but, remember, the more players, the longer it takes to complete. One year, we played the game with only four couples. Since we all knew what we and our spouses had brought, it was slim pickings that year, albeit a more controlled process. I opened a large, flat gift that turned out to be a three-foot-wide pastel watercolor print of Victorian ladies in a garden, beautifully framed and matted. Perfect for yours truly.

Then it was stolen. Waa-ah.

It was Michael's turn next. He stole it back for me.

The woman who brought the gift actually apologized for bringing the picture. Although she'd liked it when she initially bought it, she wound up never hanging it in her house—it simply didn't go with the rest of her more contemporary home.

No worries. It fit perfectly in our traditional, English-cottage-style home filled with antiques and old things. We hung it in the bedroom, and every time we look at it, we remember our friends and their fun white elephant gift exchange.

A nice variation on this game is to have a white elephant exchange of Christmas ornaments. Michael and I both did this at our respective work parties, where the ornaments came both wrapped and unwrapped. Wrapping them adds to the suspense and makes it a surprise, while leaving them unwrapped allows everyone to see all the ornaments and choose the one they like best. Great for those who have a theme to their holiday decor. Once again, stealing is limited to three times per ornament.

Speaking of work, Secret Santas are a great way to celebrate the holiday at the office or even among families. Everyone's name goes in a hat, and each person draws a name. Whatever name you get, you become that person's Secret Santa, and you're responsible for getting them small gifts—if you're in an office setting, you might leave some candy on their desk or put a box of chocolates in their mailbox. The Santas' identities are revealed on the last day of the game.

Since some people always go overboard and do too much, and others are overwhelmed and wind up doing nothing, shortchanging their coworkers, it's best to establish very specific Secret Santa guidelines. (These "rules" are meant to be freeing rather than restricting—to allow everyone to have fun and avoid hurt feelings among the recipients.

Secret Santa Guidelines
- The game starts the Monday after Thanksgiving and ends on December 21.
- Don't spend more than fifteen to twenty dollars for the entire month.
- Look for inexpensive or free things:
  - Buy stocking-stuffer-type toys.
  - Decorate the recipient's desk with Christmas bows and ribbons.
  - Leave special voicemail messages.
  - Send anonymous Christmas cards, being sure to disguise your handwriting (or simply type the note).
  - Cut festive pictures from holiday catalogs and tape them around your recipient's desk or cubicle.

- Send a holiday helium balloon.

- Have someone else—a spouse or a child—handwrite a festive note to the recipient: that way, your coworker will never recognize the handwriting.

- Give homemade or gourmet, store-bought cookies or brownies.

- Do no fewer than two things a week, and no more than three.

- Remember: keep your identity a secret from everyone so it won't spoil the surprise!

Another fun event to do during the holidays is to host a Christmas Eve open house. We did this for years, inviting both sides of the family and a few special friends. In the beginning, I went all out, offering several made-from-scratch appetizers, hearty homemade soups (prepared by Michael) accompanied by crusty breads, a fruit bowl drenched in orange curaçao, and a delicious red velvet cake with thick cream cheese icing from the local bakery. Michael's yummy carrot cake, and platters of assorted Christmas cookies, candies, and homemade fudge, along with hot apple cider and eggnog. Eventually, though, all these preparations left me feeling stressed and worn out, so I decided to scale back and go the simple fare route instead.

We switched to a single homemade appetizer, cheese and crackers, a fresh veggie platter, plump, globe grapes, two homemade soups, and crusty rolls. By then, we were "sweeted out," and the thought of gorging on cakes and fudge was too much. Instead, for those who hadn't gotten their fill of sweets yet, I set out a plate of Christmas cookies.

Afterwards, we had crackers.

Christmas crackers are a cross between a Christmas stocking and a piñata. Resembling a paper-towel tube, they're wrapped in gaily colored paper and twisted at each end like the cellophane around a piece of peppermint candy. (I've found elegant ruby-red ones made out of what looks like high-end Christmas wrapping paper foil, I love.) Inside each cracker are a couple of toys, a silly joke, and a goofy crown-shaped crepe-paper hat. To open the crackers, you pull on each end. A tiny firecracker cap inside pops, spilling the contents of the cracker onto the floor.

Christmas crackers were brought to our shores by the Brits. Once an anomaly in the US, this very English tradition has caught on here in recent years. You can now find British Christmas crackers in many stores, not just import ones.

The first time I ever pulled on an English cracker, the loud pop startled me. (It startled our dog too. Gracie ran over, barking up a storm.)

Our English friends who formerly owned a bed-and-breakfast in the Gold Country town of Sutter Creek, where we loved to stay at least once a year, explained to us that they played the crackers like a turkey wishbone. Two people each grab opposite ends of one cracker and tug until it bursts. Whoever winds up with the bigger end of the wrappings gets the toys inside.

Our friends Dave and Patricia, who live in Dorset on the south coast of England, shared their variation of the wishbone idea. Everyone stands in a circle, crossing arms in front of their chests, and tugging the crackers all at the same time. It's hilarious to see Yanks yanking on crackers this way—we still haven't gotten the hang of it. But we have fun trying.

Once the crackers are opened, everyone is required to don their crepe-paper crown and read their silly riddle aloud. One year, Michael's ninety-year-old grandmother even perched a crown on her white head and read aloud her riddle—and we have the photos to prove it.

Our friends Ryan and Ella like to do something a bit different. They try to have a solstice party each year for their friends who don't feel comfortable going to church or don't enjoy Christmas—for whatever reason. "We know they're lonely and need some cheer," Ella said, "so we'll have a simple meal of soup and bread, and the guests will bring appetizers. We don't play Christmas music, and it gives us a nice little break from all the Christmas stuff."

Hmm. Maybe Michael and I can wangle an invitation for next year.

Michael's Potato-Leek Soup

Ingredients:

- 4 tablespoons butter
- 8 cups thinly sliced leeks (see note)
- 8 cups (2 32-ounce boxes) chicken broth
- 4 large russet potatoes (unpeeled), cut into ½-inch cubes
- 2 teaspoons dried rosemary or thyme (your choice—or use a mixture of both)
- ½ teaspoon white pepper (black pepper works as a substitute)
- ½ cup heavy cream (or more, to taste)
- Salt, to taste

Note: While many people only use about half of the leek, we like to use a lot more. The stalks get tougher the higher up you go, but this soup is well-cooked and then blended, so the texture is fine. Plus, we want as much of the dark green as possible to give more color to the soup. Also, leeks are notorious for trapping sand and grit from the fields. Michael's solution is to wash, then slice them, filling the measuring cup with the desired amount. Then he washes the slices one more time in the colander, pressing them with a spoon to separate the rings. This ensures a grit-free dining experience.

Instructions:

1. Melt the butter in a large saucepan or Dutch oven over medium heat.
2. Add the leeks and cook for about 5 to 10 minutes, till softened.
3. Add broth, potatoes, and pepper, and bring to a boil.
4. Cover, reduce heat to medium-low, and simmer for about 30 minutes, or until everything is very tender.
5. Blend the soup with a stick blender or immersion blender. (You may also blend it in batches in a regular blender or food processer. Be careful to allow the steam to escape.)
6. Stir in cream.
7. Add salt and additional pepper, to taste.
8. Serve with rolls or a nice crusty bread.

12

What Happens When You <u>Can't</u> Go Home for Christmas

Christmas is a necessity. There has to be at least one day of the year to remind us that we're here for something else besides ourselves.
—Eric Sevareid

As a little girl who devoured books set in distant lands and marveled over movies showing the Eiffel Tower, Big Ben, and Michelangelo's David, I wanted to grow up to become a cosmopolitan woman and travel the world. See the sights of Europe.

That's why, after high school, I joined the air force. A few months after completing basic training in Texas, I found myself winging my way to Europe, where I was happily stationed for the next five years. Heaven. By the time I was twenty-three years old, I'd traveled to England, Scotland, Wales, Germany, the Netherlands, France, Belgium, Switzerland, Austria, Luxembourg, Liechtenstein, Italy, Greece, Denmark, and the island of Sardinia.

One Christmas—make that one Christmas dinner—in particular stands out in my memory. While I was stationed in England, my air force roommate, Diane, and I had both been invited to family events by our respective commanders. Eager to be on our own and not wanting to feel like third wheels, we politely declined these familial offers.

We agreed we'd enjoy a traditional English Christmas dinner at the village pub across the street from our 350-year-old stone cottage. After all, we were both sophisticated, independent women of the world living in a foreign country; we certainly didn't need a family to celebrate the holiday. We thought it would be much more fun and interesting to enjoy Christmas dinner in a pub with the locals.

Christmas morning, we listened to a little Nat King Cole as we exchanged gifts over a leisurely "cuppa" tea and toast and gabbed about the air force officers who had caught our eyes. (Military regulations prohibited "fraternization" between officers and enlisted servicemembers, but there were creative ways of getting around the rules.) Once we finished gushing to each other about the latest fighter pilots on base, we sauntered over to the pub just before lunchtime to enjoy a nice Christmas meal.

That's when we learned the sad truth.

"Sorry, luv, we're not serving meals today," the kindly, red-cheeked publican informed us. "We're closing up early so everyone can celebrate Christmas dinner with their families."

No meals? Not even a sausage roll? Toad in the hole (sausages baked in Yorkshire pudding)? Bubble and squeak (sausage and potatoes)?

Not one bite. The only food the pub had on the premises was an assortment of crisps (potato chips) and candy bars to satisfy our growling tummies, which were ready to erupt into a full-fledged roar. Diane chose salt-and-vinegar crisps, and I picked sour cream and onion. And for dessert? Two Kit-Kats apiece.

Diane had a much better Christmas in Germany six years later with her soon-to-be-husband, Warren. "We bought a small tree from the Christmas tree lot and decorated it with ornaments we'd bought locally and from the BX," she recalled. "We cooked a nice ham, potatoes and gravy, vegetables and salad, and bought wonderful *brochen* [rolls] from the nearby bakery and a Black Forest *gateau* [cake] for dessert. There was always something to do overseas," Diane said, "even if it was just walking along the *walkplatz* [shopping area] when the stores were closed. They always had little stands set up selling potato pancakes with applesauce, bratwurst, and *gluhwein* [warm mulled wine] at Christmastime."

I remember those food stands well. That's where I was first introduced to *pommes frites mit mayonnaise* (French fries with mayo, not ketchup) when I was stationed in Germany.

Many Decembers ago, in 1989, Michael spent Christmas on a cruise ship in the Caribbean. Not as exciting as it sounds—it was his job. He worked behind the scenes in entertainment as a stage manager, running lights and sound for the performers, and operating the movie theater and TV station on board. As a cruise ship employee, Michael was only allowed to bring four pieces of luggage on board. Naturally, that necessitated leaving all his Christmas decorations behind.

On one of its ports of call, the ship stopped in St. Thomas, one of the Virgin Islands. Michael found a Walgreens in St. Thomas with a small Christmas section and bought a few strands of lights, some tinsel garland, and an eighteen-inch fake tabletop Christmas tree with miniature ornaments.

He decorated his cabin, hanging up the lights and garland around the ceiling, doorway, desk, TV, and porthole. Other decorations were placed in strategic spots to complete the effect. The other ship employees loved it, complimenting Michael on how festive his cabin looked.

Michael and a few of his shipmates also decided to participate in Secret Santa. Three male employees drew the names of three female employees, and vice versa. Michael drew Julie, the social director. (Not to be confused with social director Julie from *The Love Boat*.) One evening, when Julie was in her cabin getting ready for dinner, Michael stealthily plastered the outside of her door with figures of Santa and his reindeer.

Surprise!

He decided to gift Julie his favorite holiday book, *The Best Christmas Pageant Ever* by Barbara Robinson. It tells the story of the Herdmans, "the worst kids in the history of the world," and how they managed to muscle their way into the leading roles of the church Christmas pageant. It's a hilarious yet poignant book that provides a fresh perspective on what it must have been like that first Christmas.

The trouble was, everyone knew how much Michael loved the book, so giving it to Julie would betray his Secret Santa identity. The solution? He bought a copy for each of his three female coworkers. No need to be secret, and this way they all benefited.

On Christmas Eve, Michael talked one of the German desk clerks into giving him the key to Julie's cabin so he could secretly deliver her stocking. (It was against the rules to give out keys to other cabins, but Michael explained the situation and what he was doing, and the German clerk readily agreed.)

Proving that not only do elves come in different sizes but also from different countries. Michael had been working all month on Julie's stocking (remember his stocking fetish?) and enjoyed imagining her surprise when she came "home" and discovered that Santa doesn't need a chimney to deliver presents.

He wasn't prepared for Julie's reaction.

Having worked until after midnight on Christmas Eve, it wasn't until Christmas morning that Julie could seek out her Secret Santa and thank him. She told Michael how much she loved her stocking, sharing that she'd sobbed when she opened the wrapped package of Scotch tape. "My mama and daddy always put Scotch tape in our stockings," Julie told him.

Proving to Michael that even though we grow up on the outside, there's still a little kid inside every one of us.

13

Rent-a-Kid and Other Ways to Make the Yuletide Bright

> *I love these little people, and it is not a slight thing when they, who are fresh from God, love us.*
> —Charles Dickens

Whether you're single or married without kids, there's something special about spending time with a child at Christmas and seeing the magic and wonder through their eyes. If you don't have a child, or your children are grown, I recommend "renting" a kid—spending one-on-one time with a niece, nephew, grandchild, neighbor, or son or daughter of a friend during the holidays.

My friend Kim shared a delightful story about her niece Mackenzie and the wonderful Christmas tradition they started when she was young. "When Mackenzie was three years old," Kim recalled, "my mom and I took her to a musical rendition of *A Christmas Carol*. The production wasn't meant for young children, however, so we got some sideways glances. One patron was even so bold as to say, 'She's so young! Are you sure she won't get bored and make a fuss?'"

"We were sure," Kim said. "I'd swear she came out of the womb adoring anything on a stage. She'd already been to a couple of other theatrical performances, and each time was the same: enthralled, eyes wide, and not a peep out of her from beginning to end. That same year—and since Mackenzie is a Christmas baby, born on December 23—I thought, 'What better way to celebrate than to take her to *The Nutcracker* ballet?' We read her the story beforehand and introduced her to all the characters. It was all she could talk about for a week. Always in the Christmas spirit, I was looking forward to a little fairy dust myself," Kim recalled.

"The evening of the performance went exactly as anticipated: enthralled, eyes wide, and not a peep from beginning to end," Kim said. "We were having so much fun, I decided on a fancy dinner afterwards to top off the evening. I ordered an appetizer of steamed mussels, never dreaming a three-year-old would want any. The next thing I knew, she'd rolled up her sleeves and was elbow-deep in the plate of mollusks! We laughed so hard we had to take a picture just to prove it to the rest of the family," Kim recounted.

"Then and there, we decided to make it a Christmas tradition—every year, I would take my niece to *The Nutcracker* and a fancy restaurant (with steamed mussels on the menu). One year we did this in San Francisco and dreamed about other cities we would eventually take our tradition to—London? Paris? Moscow? After all, the sugar plum fairy sprinkles her dust and makes Christmas magic all over the world.... Do they have mussels in Moscow?"

I don't know if they have mussels in Moscow, but I do know they have Mel's Diner in Sacramento. Mel's Diner and a matinee were usually the entertainment of choice for my nephew Josh and me during the Christmas season when he was young. We loved catching the latest children's comedy or action-adventure film at the movie theater. (For some reason, Josh wasn't too interested in sugar plum fairies.)

Josh also remembers my taking him to another '50s-style diner in our neighborhood that had Thunderbirds and other '50s cars sticking out of the walls. We'd sit in car seats inside the retro diner while we downed cheeseburgers and chocolate shakes.

Josh hasn't been a young boy for years, but he told me he remembers something about a burping contest in the car on the way home after we saw *Back to the Future* together. I'm sure he's mistaken. His aunt Laura was too genteel, too refined, too much of a lady, to do anything so gross and junior-highish as burp.

In public.

Another thing Josh liked to do around the holidays with me, his mom, and Grandma when he was young was bake Christmas cookies. Like most kids, Josh liked to make sugar-cookie cutouts he could decorate to his heart's content. I seem to remember a giant purplish-brown Santa whose head my nephew eagerly bit off before the frosting had even hardened.

There are also ways to brighten the life of a child you *don't* know during the holidays.

Every year, our church participates in a countywide program called "Gifts from the Heart," a holiday giving campaign benefitting over 3,000 foster children, disabled adults, and the elderly. Foster children and adults in the program fill out tags with the items they need or would like for Christmas. The county social workers then deliver the tags to our church a few weeks before Thanksgiving. The tags are displayed on a table in the fellowship hall after services for the congregation to choose from. We always try to select a couple of kids and seniors for whom we can be Santa Claus. Then we hit the stores.

As a rule, I don't enjoy shopping. With the exception of bookstores, I'm not a browser; I can't spend hours in a store ambling through the aisles looking at everything. In fact, early in our marriage, Michael nicknamed me "Diana, the huntress" for my single-minded ability to enter a store, go directly to the item I needed, not allowing myself to be distracted from my prey, buy it, and leave. In and out in ten minutes.

Our annual Gifts from the Heart shopping trip is a different animal altogether—the most fun we ever have shopping. We love choosing gifts for the kids—children who otherwise might not have presents under their tree, particularly if they're still waiting to be placed in a foster home. Sometimes, we'll go to Toys "R" Us to find a specific toy a child has requested; other times, we'll hit a discount department store like Ross or TJ Maxx, which always have a wide variety of choices. (These stores are great places to get children's clothes from their tags as well. Some ask for jeans or sweatshirts; others, pajamas and a robe; and still others, a warm jacket. The latter always breaks my heart, and we'll usually throw in a scarf and gloves as well for good measure.)

Our favorite things to buy for kids are books and art supplies. As someone who has loved books since childhood, I always look for tags from children who want to escape into a good book, while Michael looks for the tags from kids asking for art supplies. When we find those tags—few and far between—we snatch them up.

We head to our local bookstore, where I'll happily shop for hours, finding just the right books for the age of the children I've selected. Then it's off to Michael's favorite art store, where he's like a kid in a candy shop, choosing just the right set of paints or colored pencils and sketchbooks.

Some kids, though, only have one item on their tag: a bicycle.

Bicycles now are nothing like they were back in the Dark Ages when I was a child. Today's bikes come with all sorts of bells and whistles and can easily cost hundreds of dollars. Gulp. I'm not a parent, and my nieces and nephews are grown and out of the house, so I didn't have a clue how expensive bicycles had gotten. We leave those tags for our congregation members with deeper pockets.

This isn't the only way you can play Santa to kids, though. Many shopping malls in the community—often in conjunction with philanthropic organizations—have Christmas trees set up in the center of the mall covered with paper "ornaments" that bear the name, age, and Christmas wishes of children in the area. You can select one or more children's names from the tree, shop for the gift(s) they requested, then wrap and deliver them to the volunteers at the mall.

There are also organizations, such as The Salvation Army, which fulfill the Christmas wishes and needs of children up to twelve years old with their Angel Tree program.

One of our friends summed it up best: "This is my special time for anonymous giving," she said. "I take great pains in choosing the angels from the tree and shopping for the gifts on my own. It's also my time of reflection—a look back with thanksgiving for all the privileges and blessings I had as a child that those children don't have."

Our family had angels arrive one Christmas, too.

When I was fifteen, my dad died unexpectedly at the age of thirty-eight of a heart attack two weeks before Christmas. Suddenly, my mom was left with four kids to raise on her own. We'd just moved to Phoenix from Wisconsin a few months earlier, and even though we had relatives in this desert city from my mom's side of the family, it was hard to be in a new place at Christmas—especially without my dad. To help out, a nearby church brought over food, clothing, and gifts for me and my three siblings.

I've never forgotten their kindness.

My father was a big believer in the Golden Rule: "Do unto others as you would have them do unto you"—something he taught his four children.

Recalling this rule, several years ago, Michael and I made the decision to change our gift giving. We used to give gits to everyone in our respective families—including those we're not close to or don't see very often—but it was getting out of control.

Michael's the youngest in a family of six children, and I'm the second oldest in a family of six. All our siblings have children of their own, and most have spouses. Most of *their* kids now have kids as well. It got to the point where we were giving gifts to more than fifty family members. Yikes!

We asked our families to stop giving us gifts and said that we would do the same. Instead, we take the money we would have spent on those myriad family members to "adopt" a needy family in the community.

Michael's aunt Betty once recounted the story to us of a young woman, "Mary," who didn't have a very merry Christmas to look forward to. Her husband had left her and their two children just when she was about to give birth to her third child. He took nearly everything she owned and left her practically nothing.

It looked to be a pretty lean Christmas for Mary's family—until her coworkers rallied around the young mom. Betty's church joined in to provide a Christmas turkey and all the trimmings, as well as additional food to stock Mary's cupboards. They also gave the single mom odds and ends of furniture, a microwave, and some much-needed cash, clothes, and toys for the kids.

Mary couldn't believe it—that strangers would do all this for *her*. She told Betty she realized they were "angels." God had sent to her and her family in time of need.

Is there someone you can be an angel to this Christmas?

Christmas is doing a little something extra for someone.
—Charles Schulz

Tips for Finding a Child in Need

For further details on The Salvation Army's Angel Tree program, visit https://saangeltree.org.

If there's not a program sponsored by your local shopping mall, contact your local fire department. Local fire departments often have a Toys for Tots-type program, or would likely know of one in your area.

14

Less Isn't Always More (Deck the Halls, Part Two)

> Like snowflakes, my Christmas memories gather and dance—each beautiful, unique, and gone too soon.
> —Deborah Whipp

Although my husband may be the "crafty" one in our family—able to create something beautiful out of next to nothing—*I'm* the one who knows how to display it. I'm the decorating diva—in a good way. I love making things pretty by placing them in just the right spot, whether it's Michael's gorgeous quilts, a watercolor we brought home from England, or the vintage floral china plates I pick up at flea markets and garage sales.

I'm not a collector, though. Doesn't every civilized home have seventeen teapots?

Michael, on the other hand, is the king of collectors, and his biggest collection is of Father Christmases. While shopping at the mall in the mid-1980s, the man who would later become my husband happened upon two small ceramic figurines of Father Christmas, European with a nineteenth-century design. These old-world figures were different from all the Santa Clauses he was used to seeing. He told me they had that certain something that said they belonged in his apartment.

The next summer, Michael was on tour with his theater troupe in Colorado Springs. Wandering through the city one day in July, it was the first time he had noticed a Christmas shop open all year, so he decided to investigate.

And there it was.

A music box of Santa Claus kneeling before the Christ child in the manger, Santa's cap respectfully removed, his hands folded in prayer. Intrigued, Michael picked up the music box and wound it up. When "O Come, All Ye Faithful" started playing, he said it all clicked. Santa Claus. Saint Nicholas. Of course, a saint would worship Jesus—his adoration for the Holy One would motivate all his other actions. Although Michael could ill afford this treasure with his actor's salary, he bought the music box.

Now he had an official collection.

He wound up buying a few more Father Christmases that year, but soon decided to limit himself to one new Father Christmas a year (since too much of a good thing is still too much). That didn't stop family and friends from adding to his collection. Apart from the music box, nearly all Michael's Father Christmases are old-fashioned with an old-world look. All these years later, he still holds to his tradition of buying only one a year for himself.

When he married me, though, I got in on the tradition and bought Michael a Father Christmas every year. One year in particular stands out.

In September 2001, Michael and I took a long-awaited vacation to England, where I introduced my beloved to the land of my heart. The ancient, walled city of York was one of our favorite places; Constantine was crowned emperor of the Roman Empire there in 306 AD. York Minster is one of the world's greatest Gothic cathedrals—beautiful and majestic. We were thrilled when we got to attend an Evensong service there.

That first day in York, we decided to split up for a few hours. I needed to check email at the Internet café, and Michael wanted to do some touristy things. (Internet cafés were popular in the days before reliable mobile phone access—you paid a small hourly fee to use their computers and Internet connection.) We agreed to meet up later for teatime.

As Michael glanced through the brochure we'd picked up from the tourist information office, he spotted an ad for a shop called Christmas Angels. Open all year. "Aha," he thought. "Maybe I'll find this year's Father Christmas in his homeland—England." Seeking out the store, he browsed through it, not finding a figure he liked until he got to the back corner.

In that corner, Michael found a figurine of Father Christmas that looked as if it were from the late 1800s. Featuring two Victorian-era children on a sled, it was the most wonderful figure he'd ever seen, with an equally wonderful price tag. "Dear," as the Brits would say. Before spending that much though, he decided he'd better check with me, so he headed over to the Internet café.

I was so excited when I saw Michael. When we'd parted earlier, I hadn't gone directly to the café; instead, I'd stopped at a gift store across from York Minster where I had found the perfect Father Christmas to give my husband that year. Beaming, I handed him the bag, knowing the figure was different from any other in his collection. "Open it," I said.

Michael did, and thought it was beautiful: Father Christmas in profile in mid-stride wearing a sky-blue cloak. Unfortunately, I hadn't noticed that Father Christmas's hat was broken. When we went back to the store to exchange the figurine for one that wasn't broken, Michael saw what a bargain it was, thus escalating the extravagance of the one he'd found. Still hoping, he invited me to check out Christmas Angels. We made our way to the back corner of the shop. When I saw the Victorian Father Christmas on the sled with the two children, I fell in love with it, as well, and agreed this figure was the one Michael should buy that year.

Then I saw the price.

"Well, it's English as English can be," I said.

"And it's from York," Michael added.

"It's fabulous," I said.

"Isn't it?"

Pause.

"It needs to be in your collection."

Michael did an inner fist pump.

Once the shop clerk placed this treasure in the protective Styrofoam container inside its original box, however, we realized there was no way it would fit in our luggage. We decided to ship it home. The clerk didn't know what the exact shipping cost would be, and since it was late on a Saturday afternoon, he couldn't call anyone to find out, but we went ahead and made the arrangements anyway.

When we got our credit card bill, we discovered that the shipping cost exceeded the price of Father Christmas.

Are we sorry we bought it? No way. Are we sorry we didn't make room for it in our luggage? Definitely.

While this Father Christmas from York turned out to be the most expensive in Michael's collection, it's no match in sentimental value for the trio his mother made for him.

During our first year of marriage, late one November afternoon, Michael and I were unpacking some Christmas boxes he'd had in storage. Opening one box marked "Fragile," he carefully pulled out the large figurines.

"These were powder when Mom started making them," he explained. "She mixed and poured the slip [liquid clay] and fired them in her own kiln." He showed me the one with the flowing coat of sapphire blue, and the biggest one, with the reindeer, pointing out his mother's attention to detail, particularly the eyes. "The mark of true artistry and craftsmanship is the eyes," Michael said.

Then he pulled out the Father Christmas clad in dark green. The lines were not as crisp, the eyes fuzzy—obviously painted with a shaking hand. "That's when Mom was sick," Michael said. His mother had been ill for years. In fact, the doctors had given her just weeks, "maybe months," to live, and that had been four years earlier.

What a memorable afternoon that was, hearing my new husband reminisce about his mom, his family, and holidays past. Then we went over to dinner at a friend's house. When we got home (in those pre-cell phone days) we learned Michael's mom had passed away that very evening. He told me he'll always be grateful that at the end of his mother's life on earth, he was sharing wonderful memories of her with me.

Thanks to his collection.

That first Christmas together, when Michael pulled out box after box of Father Christmases, I was overwhelmed, to say the least. Where in the world were we going to display all of these figures in our one-bedroom apartment?

Never fear. My decorating diva gene kicked in, and I covered every imaginable surface with Father Christmases—bookcases, kitchen counters, end tables…I even put a trio representing different countries on the back of the commode.

And every time I flushed, I thought I detected the faint hum of bagpipes.

When we moved into our own house, I thought that we would finally have enough room for all of our combined Christmas decorations.

Not exactly.

In those years before our move, Michael's Father Christmas collection had multiplied like rabbits, so we were still hard-pressed to display them all. The good news is that we've now instituted a new tradition of starting our holiday decorating the day after Thanksgiving, giving me plenty of time to squeeze the white-bearded guy into every nook and cranny before December 25.

One year, I decided I wanted an elegant mantel like the one I'd seen in a home decorating magazine—nothing but fresh Christmas greenery and ivory candles in varying shapes and sizes. I imagined how beautiful it would look with all the candles lit as the scent of evergreen wafted through the house.

Michael nixed my idea, saying he was "uncomfortable" with lit candles near highly flammable Christmas boughs. His worry was probably warranted, but it could also have stemmed from his memory of the year he lit his grandmother's mantel on fire when he tried to put a tabletop Christmas tree into the crackling fireplace. One of the tree branches caught on the metal fireplace screen and exploded in a shower of flames that shot as high as the five-foot mantel, igniting the boughs on top and sending flames licking their way up. In less than three seconds, there were flames from floor to ceiling. Michael, a high-school sophomore at the time, stood there, saying, "Oh. Oh. Oh."

Now he was telling me, "No. No. No."

I didn't understand why I couldn't have the pretty candles I wanted. After all, no serious damage had occurred at his grandmother's house, and the insurance had paid for the repairs.

But Michael was insistent. "You can have either unlit candles and real boughs, or lit candles and fake boughs. But you *cannot* have real boughs and lit candles." On this he refused to budge.

So much for my elegant decorating dreams that year. After mourning the loss of my pretty mantel vision for a few days, I went out and bought some artificial greenery that never caught on fire.

One Christmas season a few years into our marriage, Michael decided to sell some of his projects at holiday craft fairs. His biggest hit—in addition to the pearl beaded ornaments—were two-foot-square quilted wall hangings of Christmas trees or wreaths. Everyone who stopped by his booth oohed and aahed over Michael's intricate work, and our family members eyed these wall hangings covetously. That year, several members of our immediate family—along with a couple of dear friends—received a quilted wall hanging for Christmas.

It was only afterward that I realized our home didn't have one of the wreath hangings. That crafty guy of mine remedied the omission in short order. Michael had seven leftover individual wreath panels he hadn't yet made into completed wall hangings. Wanting to do something special for me, he dashed off two more wreath "tops" on the sewing machine and stitched all nine together to form one giant wall hanging.

I'm grateful every day to be married to such a talented Renaissance man.

One of the Christmas decorations that means the most to me is a twelve-inch "jewel tree" my mother made years ago in the style of those crafted by her mother-in-law, my grandma Florence. As a child, I was continually transfixed by the way Grandma Florence's jewel trees sparkled and glittered in the light. She would craft the trees using bits and pieces of mismatched costume jewelry she kept in an old cigar box—a rhinestone earring here, a faux garnet brooch there, a pretend sapphire that had long ago fallen out of its ring setting—all mixed together with imitation pearls and gleaming beads from broken necklaces. Grandma would affix these pretty gems and jewels to a Styrofoam cone with straight pins and glue, constantly turning the cone to make sure every bit of

Styrofoam was covered. For the base of her creations, she'd spray paint a small, ice-cream sundae glass gold, then glue the glittering tree to the top.

My grandma made jewel trees for both of her daughters and daughters-in-law, but she passed away before she had a chance to make any for her granddaughters, including me. Lisa and I would have been too young to appreciate them at the time. Years later, though, when we were older, my mom painstakingly made us each a jewel tree following Grandma Florence's pattern. They were a thing of beauty. Every Christmas, I would set mine out and admire the pretty stones sparkling in the light, and think of my grandmother and my mom.

Thanks, Mom.

Michael really liked the jewel tree from my mother as well—so much so, in fact, that he started collecting old jewelry to one day make a tree of his own.

Sadly, over the years, Mom's jewel tree has lost some of its luster, and some of its beads—probably from the repeated wrapping and unwrapping every Christmas. Even after Michael replaced the beads for me, the tree still didn't sparkle as brightly as it once did. I decided to stop putting it away with the Christmas decorations every year and to display it permanently on a bookcase in our bedroom.

A few years ago, Michael had to have shoulder replacement surgery. After the surgery, he was unable to sleep in a bed and slept in his recliner in the den instead. Many nights, though, sleep proved elusive. While I slept, Michael went into his studio at the back of the house, shut the door, and started making that jewel Christmas tree he'd been wanting to create for years.

He ended up making not just one but three jewel trees, all of them drop-dead gorgeous, with rhinestones, imitation rubies, emeralds, sapphires, and even antique watch faces. I love them.

Every year when I decorate now, I place the "jewel-tree forest" on a silver tray on the buffet in front of the mirror, a candle illuminating the gems and reflecting their sparkle in the mirror.

Loving decorating as I do, and being married to Mr. Christmas himself, I like to go all out for this holiday, ignoring the "less is more" effect I aim for the rest of the year. (All right, friends and family members—and anyone who's ever set foot in our home—you can stop laughing now.)

One November, though, I was approaching a major book deadline, Michael was busy with a play, and neither of us had the energy for our annual decorating decathlon. That year, we opted for the less-is-more look and scaled way back. We still put up a tree—two, in fact; the elegant one in the living room and the fun one in the den—but we reduced the Father Christmas collection to Michael's top ten favorites. The only other decoration was the nativity set and a fresh evergreen wreath on the front door.

That year, we enjoyed a nice, peaceful Christmas. I wasn't frantic or hurried, and it wasn't a major decoration production that took more than a week to accomplish. The next year, though, we found we'd missed seeing all our treasures, so we hauled the myriad plastic tubs of holiday decorations down from the garage rafters.

Patricia, our English friend, tells of the time she and her family went out for a special meal during the holidays. "The paper Christmas napkins were gorgeous," she recalled, "so my sister-in-law swiped some from another table and put them in her handbag. They were a little creased by the time she got them home, so she ironed them. I think she was probably a little the worse for wear," Patricia said with a smile, "because she did this on the carpet. As a result, she had to move the furniture around to cover a curious patch of blurred holly leaves and berries."

Hmmm. Carpet decorating. That's one area of the house I hadn't considered embellishing.

Decorating Tip

If you're from the less-is-more school of decorating, Christmas may be the time to let your inner clutter bug out. Be free! Go wild and crazy!

And if you can't go crazy, stick with simple instead and only display the things that mean the most to you, even if it's just evergreen boughs and candles on the mantel. Remember to use artificial boughs, though, if you want to light the candles. (Or use flameless LED candles with real boughs. Easy-peasy.)

15

Sing Out! A Totally Subjective List of Favorite Christmas Music

Where words fail, music speaks.
—Hans Christian Andersen

Christmas music is such a huge part of the season, I thought it would be fun to include a chapter of favorite holiday music—sung by whoever the Walker household thinks sings it the best. (My husband Michael, a trained singer back in the day, and I don't always agree.) This won't be an exhaustive list; my selections will be based on the CD collection in our house.

Yes, we still have CDs. We're old. But we do have playlists on our phones now, too, so I've added some of those choices as well.

I hope you enjoy our random Christmas music list, split into categories: classic, contemporary, and novelty.

Favorite Classic Christmas Songs

"White Christmas": Gotta be Bing Crosby. His version is the top-selling holiday single of all time. Runner-up: Bing's duet with Rosemary Clooney.

"Silver Bells": also goes to Bing and Rosemary. It's rich, it's warm, it's classic. (Note: "Silver Bells" debuted in Bob Hope's 1951 movie *The Lemon Drop Kid*. In my film critic opinion, that song was the best thing about the movie.)

"The Christmas Song (Chestnuts Roasting on an Open Fire)": Nat King Cole, of course. Nat was the first person to record this song, and his version is arguably the best. A close second is Linda Eder, someone you might not have heard of, but she's a former Broadway star whom we've seen in concert twice, and she's a huge hit in our house. Her voice is out of this world—a bit of Barbra Streisand, a bit of Celine Dion, and just enough Linda Ronstadt.

"Have Yourself a Merry Little Christmas": Judy Garland. It's worth watching all of *Meet Me in St. Louis* just to see a wistful Judy in that gorgeous red velvet dress sing this song.

Second-place tie: Linda Ronstadt and Rosemary Clooney.

"I'll Be Home for Christmas": Linda Ronstadt. She has a way with those '40s ballads.

"Silent Night": split decision. For Michael, it used to be opera diva Kathleen Battle, but now she's been surpassed by Linda Eder. For me, it's Barbra Streisand all the way.

"Do You Hear What I Hear?": Linda Eder, hands down. (Linda got her start on Broadway in *Jekyll and Hyde*.) With its *Lion King* orchestration and choir background, crank it up so you can *feel* the song tonight. Always gives me chills. Josh Groban and Bing Crosby are tied for second.

"O Holy Night": Celine Dion. Simple and pure. There's no one like Celine. I remember Julie Andrews doing a beautiful rendition of this song back in the day, but we didn't have it in our collection, so I can't officially list Julie.

"Joy to the World": Julie Andrews. (I can list her this time since we have this one on CD.) A close second has to be Andy Williams. I grew up watching Andy's Christmas specials, so he has a nostalgic place in my heart.

"What Child Is This?": Tie between Josh Groban and Charlotte Church. A young singing sensation from Wales, teenage Charlotte with the grown-up voice became famous in the late '90s singing classical music like *Pie Jesu*. After hearing her sing for the first time, you may be asking yourself, "What child is *this?*"

"The First Noel": John McDermott, another of The Irish Tenors, with Josh Groban a close second.

"Hark! The Herald Angels Sing": For me, it's a tie between Frank Sinatra and Amy Grant. For Michael, the cast of *A Charlie Brown Christmas*.

"I Wonder as I Wander": Tie. Barbara Streisand and Linda Ronstadt.

"Ave Maria": This was a tough one. Recorded by nearly everyone who's ever done a Christmas album, the song works best with someone who's classically trained. That's why we love it sung so exquisitely by Kathleen Battle. And Placido Domingo, Mario Lanza, Andrea Bocelli, and Ronan Tynan from The Irish Tenors.

Favorite Contemporary Christmas Songs

"Let It Snow": I couldn't decide between Steve Lawrence and Eydie Gormé's delightful duet or classic Dean Martin, so I'm calling it a tie.

"Little Drummer Boy": Anne Murray

"Mary, Did You Know?": A Tie between Kathy Mattea and Pentatonix.

"Christmas Through Your Eyes": Gloria Estefan

"Merry Christmas, Darling": Karen Carpenter. There was no voice like Karen Carpenter's with that distinctive, lush contralto. In the 1970s, Paul McCartney said she had "the best female voice in the world."

"Toyland": Doris Day all the way. I love her voice and have been a fan since childhood, when I first heard her sing "Secret Love" in *Calamity Jane*.

"Song for a Winter's Night": Sarah McLachlan. Absolutely gorgeous. As is Sarah's version with The Canadian Tenors.

"Wintersong": Sarah McLachlan

"O Little Town of Bethlehem": Amy Grant. Although the lyrics are classic, her music is contemporary. We have recordings of two other melodies—Amy's is the best.

"Angels We Have Heard on High": Michael W. Smith. A rewrite of the classic. He calls it "Gloria," but a rose by any other name….

"No Eye Has Seen": Duet with Amy Grant and Michael W. Smith. Instead of the usual melody and harmony, they're singing two different songs in one, overlapping as they weave in and out with the choral background. Glorious.

"The Prayer": Charlotte Church and Josh Groban. Not exactly a "holiday" song, but it was originally recorded by Celine Dion and Andrea Bocelli for Celine's Christmas album. Although we have all four of their CDs, we think Josh and Charlotte sing the song best. More passion. More purity.

"The Bells of St. Paul's": Linda Eder. Really a remembrance of a past love, this song is set at Christmastime in London. Gorgeous. Worth the whole price of the CD.

"Sleigh Ride": Amy Grant. We've listened to and loved Amy's rendition in our house for years. (Did anyone even record it before

Amy?) Recently, though, Michael downloaded a version by Vince Gill that we're also enjoying.

"River": Joni Mitchell made this famous, and I love the folk singer's rendition, but a close second is a tie between Linda Ronstadt and Michael Ball. (Michael was the original Marius in the London West End production of *Les Misérables*.)

"Celebrate Me Home": Jennifer Nettles. Jennifer's a singer I've only discovered in the last few years. I also love her singing "Merry Christmas with Love" and "Circle of Love."

"Nothing But a Child": Kathy Mattea

"Where Are You Christmas": Faith Hill. (From *Dr. Seuss' How the Grinch Stole Christmas*.)

"Breath of Heaven": Amy Grant. Although, if our niece Jennie had recorded it, she would have easily bumped Amy. (See chapter 5, "Those Not-so-Silent Nights.")

Favorite Novelty Christmas Songs

"I Saw Mommy Kissing Santa Claus": Wayne Newton. Yes, Wayne Newton, the guy who made "Danke Schoen" famous. (Showing my age here.)

"Rudolph the Red-Nosed Reindeer": Tie between Gene Autry and Burl Ives.

"Santa Claus Is Coming to Town": Frank Sinatra. Cool. Big band swing.

"The Twelve Days of Christmas": John Denver and the Muppets. Although this is a traditional Christmas song, when performed by this bunch, it's a novelty. (Miss Piggy steals the show with her "five golden rings.")

"Baby, It's Cold Outside": Dean Martin's version is the most definitive, but I love the duet between Dolly Parton and Rod Stewart as well.

"Chipmunk Song (Christmas Don't Be Late)": Alvin and the Chipmunks. Had to list it.

"The Chimney Song": From the *Twisted Christmas* CD. Sung by a little girl about ten years old. Something's stuck in the chimney…it turns out to be Santa.

The two favorite Christmas albums in our house? Linda Eder's *Christmas Stays the Same* and Linda Ronstadt's *A Merry Little Christmas*. If you like listening to glorious female voices, these two can't be beat.

16

Attaboy, Clarence

(A "DEFINITIVE" HOLIDAY MOVIE GUIDE)

*George Bailey says, "Attaboy, Clarence," when the angel Clarence gets his wings at the end of *It's a Wonderful Life*.

> I wish we could put up some of the Christmas spirit in jars
> and open a jar of it every month.
> —Harlan Miller

Who doesn't love Christmas movies? Unless they're a Grinch or don't celebrate the holiday. Fair enough. For the rest of us, though, here's a helpful holiday movie guide.

So much more than a list, this guide includes brief plot descriptions of many Christmas films, personal anecdotes and observations, and fun movie trivia.

There are way too many movies to list, so, for the sake of simplification, I'll break them down into categories: classics (pre-1960), modern-day masterpieces, animated movies, movies set at

Christmastime that aren't necessarily *about* Christmas, and lesser-known gems.

Some films fit more than one category, so I organized them in the way that made the most sense to me. Check if your favorite made the list!

Classic Christmas Movies

It's a Wonderful Life (1946)

This movie often comes in at no. 1 on many people's best Christmas movies lists. With Jimmy Stewart as the star, that's no surprise. Jimmy was the classic everyman we could all relate to. The boy next door who became a good and decent man—one who always did the right thing and put others before himself. Also, *It's a Wonderful Life* includes one of the most romantic scenes of any movie.

Mary, played by Donna Reed, has had a crush on George since she was a little girl, even whispering into his bad ear when he was young, "George Bailey, I'll love you til the day I die." Years later, when George and the grown-up Mary share a phone receiver as they listen to their friend Sam Wainwright explain his latest money-making scheme, you can see the chemistry between the couple build. It's Something George tries to resist, insisting to Mary that he wants to see the world and never get married. Ever.

Love had other plans.

I swoon every time I watch this scene.

Fun Facts:

- This was Jimmy Stewart's first film after his return from military service, and he was nervous about the kissing scene with Donna Reed. Director Frank Capra had the idea of having them both talk on the same phone together. It worked. What we see in the film was their first take.

♦ Lionel Barrymore, crippled with arthritis, was perfect for the role of Mr. Potter, so the character gets wheeled around the set in the wheelchair. Perfect solution.

Miracle on 34th Street (1947)

A well-known New York storefront plays a prominent role in another of our most-loved Christmas movies, *Miracle on 34th Street*. Michael and I were delighted years ago when we visited the Big Apple for the first time and got to walk by Macy's on the corner of that iconic avenue.

We both grew up with this delightful black-and-white Maureen O'Hara/Natalie Wood classic, and it will forever hold a nostalgic place in our hearts. My favorite part comes near the end of the movie when little Susan (Natalie) doesn't get the Christmas present she asked for—a house in the country. She's sitting in the car, disconsolate, woodenly repeating the refrain, "I believe, I believe. It's silly, but I believe," when suddenly she screams out to her mom (Maureen O'Hara) and her mother's love interest (John Payne), who's driving, "Stop the car!"

Susan bolts out of the car and races up the front steps of the charming house she's always dreamed of—with a swing in the backyard, no less—which she asked Santa for, and which just happens to be for sale. (The wooden cane in the corner confirms it was Kris Kringle who made her dream come true.)

Don't you just love sappy, happy endings? I do—especially at Christmastime.

White Christmas (1954)

Everyone has their own favorite Christmas movie, often finding it difficult to narrow it down to just one. Not me. *White Christmas* tops my list. How can you go wrong with Bing Crosby and Rosemary Clooney singing and Danny Kaye and Vera Ellen dancing and looking gorgeous in the process? Four entertainers at the top of their game.

I've loved that movie since I first watched it with my family as a little girl in Wisconsin. My sister and I would pretend we were the Haynes sisters and perform "Sisters" in the living room, wishing we had those blue-feathered fans. (When she got older, my sister wouldn't deign to do the number with me at the holiday, so one year I roped my little brother Timmy into performing it with me instead. I clapped my mom's wig on my brother's head, stuck one of my party dresses over his t-shirt and pants, and christened him "Timothea.")

Timothea's debut performance was also his last.

Fun Fact:

- Bing Crosby and Rosemary Clooney never recorded the song "White Christmas" together. Bing and Rosemary were contracted with rival music studios, so there was no official movie soundtrack album as a result. Both of them recorded albums that included "White Christmas," but they never sang it as a duet on a record until they performed the song years later on a TV show together.

The Bishop's Wife (1947)

While the 1996 remake, *The Preacher's Wife*, with Whitney Houston's singing is fabulous, this is the original, starring Cary Grant, Loretta Young, and David Niven.

The one and only Cary sets hearts aflutter with his portrayal of the angel Dudley, who comes down from heaven in answer to a bishop's (David Niven) prayer for divine guidance as he struggles to raise funds for a new cathedral. Dudley's true identity is known only to the bishop. Everyone else thinks he's the bishop's new assistant, including the bishop's wife (Loretta Young). Angel Dudley shakes things up in ways the bishop couldn't have imagined in this romantic fantasy comedy.

A Christmas Carol (various versions and years)

A Christmas Carol can, and should, be a category unto itself. Arguably the most remade story of all time, at least one of the versions consistently makes it onto virtually everyone's Top Ten list. A quick Google search pulled up more than thirty-five different versions. Some are classic dramas, some are modern, some are comedies, some are musicals, some are animated, but all are based on the same Dickens novel.

The first American adaptation was a fifteen-minute silent film made in 1908 with Tom Rickets starring as Ebenezer Scrooge. Unfortunately, no known copies of the film exist, so it's officially considered lost.

The first "talkie" was the 1938 version, starring Reginald Owen as Scrooge. The role was originally intended for Lionel Barrymore, who played Scrooge every year on the radio, but the great actor was unable to do the role due to his arthritis (see my notes on *It's a Wonderful Life*). You can, however, hear Barrymore in the opening narration.

Fun Fact:

- The Cratchits were played by the real-life married couple Gene and Kathleen Lockhart. Their only child, June Lockhart, played one of the Cratchit children. Although most famous for playing Maureen Robinson in the original *Lost in Space* TV series from the '60s, June also had a scene-stealing part as the lovely Lucille Ballard in *Meet Me in St. Louis*.

1951's Alastair Sim film is often on the Top Ten lists as the definitive version. A British film, it was called *Scrooge* in the UK but was renamed *A Christmas Carol* for its American release.

Fun Fact:

- It was supposed to premiere at Radio City Music Hall, but management decided it was too grim for the Christmas season, so it opened elsewhere.

George C. Scott's 1984 made-for-TV version also often hits the Top Ten. Rather than depicting Scrooge as the usual miser, this version has him more as a ruthless businessman. Scott received an Emmy nomination for his portrayal.

Another frequent Top Ten lister is 1999's version with Patrick Stewart, of *Star Trek: The Next Generation* fame. The supporting cast includes some heavy hitters, including Richard E. Grant (Bob Cratchit), Joel Grey (Spirit of Christmas Past), Dominic West (Fred), and Celia Imrie (Mrs. Bennett).

Then there are the adaptations. Though not often on people's list of favorites, *An American Christmas Carol* (1979) has Henry Winkler playing Benedict Slade. It was wonderful seeing The Fonz from *Happy Days* playing a serious role, using the acting chops he honed at the Yale School of Drama, where he earned his MFA.

The 1970s *Scrooge*, starring Albert Finney, had the tagline, "What the dickens have they done to Scrooge?" This film also often tops the list for people's favorite version of *A Christmas Carol*.

Fun Fact:

- Two years earlier, another Dickens musical adaptation, *Oliver!*, won six Academy Awards, including Best Picture. Many of the sets at Shepperton Studios were also used in the filming of Scrooge.

Another musical adaptation is the wonderful *The Muppet Christmas Carol* (1992), starring Michael Caine, who is famously quoted as saying, "I'm going to play this movie like I'm working with the Royal Shakespeare Company. I will never wink, I will never do anything Muppety. I am going to play Scrooge as if it is an utterly dramatic role and there are no puppets around me."

Then there's the dark comedy *Scrooged* (1988), starring Bill Murray and a stellar supporting cast, including Karen Allen, John Forsythe, Robert Mitchem, and Alfre Woodard in the Bob Cratchit role.

Fun Fact:

- Carol Kane is hysterical as the Ghost of Christmas Present. She was supposed to have a dance double for the ballet scenes until one of the crew saw the actress rehearsing the dance scene and convinced the director to film Kane's "horrible dancing," which made it into the film.

Lest we neglect animated versions, we must include *Mr. Magoo's Christmas Carol* (1962), which is also a musical and was many a child's introduction to the classic story. Jim Backus (Thurston Howell III from *Gilligan's Island*) provides the voice for Magoo, who is on his way to a theater to play Ebenezer Scrooge in a Broadway musical of *A Christmas Carol* and, because of his nearsightedness, arrives late. And so, the mayhem begins.

Fun Fact:

- This was the first animated Christmas show created specifically for TV.

The Man Who Invented Christmas (2017) is a wonderful adaptation about the writing of *A Christmas Carol*. Starring Dan Stevens (the scrumptious Matthew Crawley—Mary's first husband—from *Downton Abbey*) as Charles Dickens, whose characters interact with him as he's writing the novel. As an author, I totally related, as my characters often speak to me and redirect the plans I had for their stories. Christopher Plummer is perfect as Ebenezer Scrooge.

Arguably the best recent adaptation is the 2022 musical comedy *Spirited*, starring Ryan Reynolds in the Scrooge role. Reynolds is reported to be one of the nicest men in Hollywood, and it's obvious the actor had too much fun playing the part of a heartless character. Will Ferrell plays Christmas Present and is constantly foiled by Reynolds. Hysterical, especially for musical theater geeks, it features songs by Benj Pasek and Justin Paul, who brought us *La La Land* and *The Greatest Showman*, and fabulous choreography and dancing—the production numbers are some of the best. Octavia Spencer, who won a well-deserved Academy Award for *The Help*, is wonderful in the Bob Cratchit-inspired character. Who knew she could sing? Her ballad, "View from Up Here," is especially beautiful.

There are so many inside jokes, you'll need to see the movie multiple times. One of my favorite scenes is when Will Ferrell's character sees someone dressed in a Buddy the Elf costume and says, "You look stupid." Another inside joke is that all the characters are clearly aware they are in a musical. What a clever idea. Michael saw this at a friend's house and insisted I see it. We subscribed to Apple TV specifically to watch this. Well worth it. Be sure to watch it all the way through to the end of the credits for a special treat.

Favorite Modern-Day Masterpieces

A Christmas Story (1983)

In our house, Christmas movie season officially kicks off on Thanksgiving night. After stuffing ourselves full of turkey, mashed potatoes and gravy, cranberry sauce, sweet potatoes, homemade stuffing, broccoli casserole, and green beans, we curl up in front of the TV in the evening with pumpkin pie and whipped cream to watch the classic *A Christmas Story*, or, as we simply call it, "Ralphie."

The hilarious tale of a young Midwestern boy and his quest to get a BB gun for Christmas—as Ralphie says, "an official Red Ryder carbine action two hundred shot range model air rifle with a compass in the stock and this thing that tells time," is chock-full of great lines we quote at random throughout the year:

"Randy lay there like a slug. It was his only defense."

"I can't put my arms down!"

"Meatloaf, smeatloaf, double-beatloaf. I hate meatloaf."

"It's a major award."

"'Fra-GEE-leh.' ['Fragile.'] Must be Italian."

"You'll shoot your eye out!"

This delightful film, set in the 1940s and based on Jean Shepherd's memoir *In God We Trust: All Others Pay Cash*, provides plenty of laughs, moments of poignancy, and a nostalgic look back at a simpler time.

Fun Facts:

- The movie was filmed in Cleveland, Ohio, while I was living there in the early eighties. My friend and former roommate Amy's brother, Jimmy, played the Cowardly Lion during Ralphie's visit to Santa at Higbee's Department Store.
- For the frozen flagpole sequence, Flick's tongue sticks not because of the ice but by vacuum. The props department drilled a hole, unseen by the camera, and rigged up a vacuum. Voilà! Just like putting your hand against the nozzle of a Shop-Vac.
- The BB gun description, as quoted by Ralphie, is an integral part of the plot; however, it contained an error: the Daisy BB Gun Company made no such model. Thanks to the film, BB gun sales skyrocketed, so Daisy created a model to match the dialogue. Talk about life imitating art.

I always enjoy seeing the opening of *A Christmas Story* with its Higbee's window scene. Higbee's was a great department store in downtown Cleveland when I lived there. I've shopped there—when I could afford it—and had a dear friend and former roommate who worked there and got to help fashion the fabulous window displays.

Love, Actually (2003)

One of our favorites. We watch it at least twice a year. For mature audiences only, it includes some nudity and strong language. We find it charming, clever, warm, and, at times, heartbreaking. (The scene where Emma Thompson's character realizes her husband, played by Alan Rickman, has been unfaithful is a master class in acting. Makes me cry every time.) Set during the six weeks leading up to Christmas, this film is a masterpiece of cinema editing. The movie weaves together ten different storylines with over twenty main characters and is practically a who's who of British film actors.

Fun Facts:

- This film started as ideas for two separate movies. Writer/director Richard Curtis had one story in mind about a prime minister falling for his employee and another story about a writer falling for his housekeeper. He decided instead to bring together all of his good ideas into one movie.
- The hat Keira Knightley's character wears when she goes to the home of her new husband's best friend in search of her wedding video had a practical purpose: then-teenage Knightley had a pimple (or spot, as the Brits would say) on her forehead that could not be concealed with makeup. Costumers added a hat, and Bob's your uncle.
- Olivia Olson, who played young Sam's crush, Joanna, did her own singing on "All I Want for Christmas," but she nailed

it all too well. Director Richard Curtis had her recording edited to make her voice sound more childlike.

- The movie soundtrack was oddly released without Olivia Olson's version of the song, as well as without Bill Nighy's version of "Christmas Is All Around." What were they thinking?
- The Rowan Atkinson character was originally supposed to be an omniscient angel, woven throughout the movie. That makes more sense as to why he was delaying Alan Rickman's Harry from buying the gold necklace and later distracting the ticket agent so Sam could sneak past him into the airline terminal. (Considered one of England's finest comic actors, Rowan Atkinson is famous for the British TV program *Mr. Bean* and the film series *Johnny English*.)

Elf (2003)

Buddy, a six-foot-tall human, finds out he's not really an elf after all and travels from the North Pole to meet his biological father. (I confess that I wasn't a Will Ferrell fan until I watched *Elf*.)

Fun Facts:

- Director Jon Favreau has a cameo role as the doctor who does the blood test to confirm Buddy is indeed Walter's biological son.
- During filming, James Caan was having trouble being mean to the other actors and asked Favreau for help. The director told him, "You're James effing Caan." That did the trick, and the next take was perfect.
- Jovie's part was not originally written as a singing part; however, Zooey Deschanel was such a fine singer that the script was adjusted accordingly.

- Will Ferrell's now-famous line "Santa! I know him!" was reportedly improvised, not scripted. Brilliant.

Home Alone (1990)

How in the world can parents fly to Europe and not know they've forgotten their eight-year-old son? This John Hughes and Chris Columbus collaboration makes it not only believable but funny. Macauley Culkin as the abandoned Kevin steals the show, and became a household name after the movie's release.

Side note: During a dentist appointment a few weeks before Christmas, I asked my new young dentist to name his favorite Christmas movie. He thought for a moment and said, *"Home Alone."*

"Not *White Christmas* or *It's a Wonderful Life?*" I asked.

"Never heard of them," he said.

Color me old.

The Holiday (2006)

Cameron Diaz, Kate Winslet, Jude Law, and Jack Black star in this house-swapping love story set in my beloved England and L.A. I've never been a Cameron Diaz fan, but I adore Kate Winslet—one of my favorite English actresses, up there with Judi Dench, Maggie Smith, Helen Mirren, and the sublime Emma Thompson. (All "Dames" of Britain, by the way.) And Jude Law? Oh, my. Who wouldn't fall for him? As someone who'd never seen any Jack Black comedies, I couldn't envision him as a romantic lead for Kate. I wasn't expecting much, but the actor surprised me. Like Kate, I'd have fallen for his character as well.

Every woman I know adores this romantic comedy. (Is it Jude Law, or that gorgeous English cottage in the countryside? For me, the English cottage wins out. Sorry, Jude.)

Not-so-Fun Fact:

+ That charming English cottage I—and countless women—love doesn't exist. Jude Law said the director "hired a field and had someone build it," bursting many bubbles in the process.

National Lampoon's Christmas Vacation (1989)

This third installment in the *Vacation* franchise is another John Hughes creation, this one telling the story of Clark Griswold just trying to have a good, old-fashioned Christmas with his family. But of course, everything goes awry.

Fun Facts:

+ Recognize the Griswolds' son? Yep, that's Johnny Galecki (Leonard of *The Big Bang Theory* fame).
+ The film still inspires various Christmas decorations and light displays. It's hard to drive around neighborhoods without seeing a "Griswold house."

Favorite Animated Christmas Movies

A Charlie Brown Christmas (1965)

It's hard to imagine anyone not loving this Christmas staple.

Fun Facts:

+ This was the first animated TV special based on the *Peanuts* comic strips.
+ Unlike the other TV animation of its day, this special does not include a laugh track.
+ Producers and the TV network thought it would be a disaster, but Charles Schulz and the team proved them wrong, winning both an Emmy and a Peabody Award.

- It was shown on US network television annually for fifty-six years before becoming exclusively available on streaming services.

How the Grinch Stole Christmas! (1966)
The best Christmas villain since Ebenezer Scrooge.

Fun Facts:
- The film was directed by Chuck Jones, most famous for the *Looney Tunes* cartoons.
- There wasn't a true script, since it's simply a narration of the book by Dr. Seuss. The story is mostly told visually.
- Boris Karloff, the narrator, is most famous for portraying Frankenstein's monster in the 1930s.
- Thurl Ravenscroft, who sang the song "You're a Mean One, Mister Grinch," also voiced Tony the Tiger in the Frosted Flakes commercials, as well as did voice-overs at various Disneyland attractions, including The Haunted Mansion, Pirates of the Caribbean, and the Disneyland Railroad.

Rudolph the Red-Nosed Reindeer (1964)
Of all the Rankin and Bass films, *Rudolph* is often considered the finest. (Of course it is. Where else can you get Burl Ives singing "Silver and Gold" and Clarice, the doe, with her long eyelashes singing, "There's Always Tomorrow"? As a kid, I'd sing along with Clarice and bat my eyes.)

The Polar Express (2004)
In this film adaptation of the book by Chris Van Allsburg, a young boy is invited aboard a mysterious train bound for the North Pole on Christmas Eve. He and the other children journey to visit Santa Claus. A solid performance from Tom Hanks. How wholesome can you get?

Fun Facts:

- The film was written, produced, and directed by Robert Zemeckis, of *Back to the Future* and *Forrest Gump* fame.
- To create this movie, a new animation process was developed: human actors were filmed using motion capture equipment, and then their movements were animated.
- Tom Hanks played six different characters: Hero Boy, Hero Boy's Father, Conductor, Hobo, the Ebenezer Scrooge puppet, and Santa Claus.
- This was the last performance of Tony Award-winning actor Michael Jeter, who died before the film's completion. It is dedicated to his memory.
- The book and film have inspired real-life train rides in various places in the US, Canada, and the United Kingdom.

The Nightmare Before Christmas (1993)

Tim Burton's blending of Halloween and Christmas, with music by Danny Elfman, tops many people's list. (Not mine, though; I don't like skeletons.)

Fun Facts:

- *The Nightmare Before Christmas* is widely regarded as one of the finest animated films of all time.
- This was the first ever animated film to be nominated for a Best Visual Effects Academy Award. It lost to *Jurassic Park*.

Arthur Christmas (2011)

James McAvoy, Hugh Laurie, Bill Nighy, Jim Broadbent, and Imelda Staunton voice the members of the Claus family in this charming story of misadventure in the world of their toy delivery service. Somehow, we missed *Arthur Christmas* when it first came out, not discovering it until last year. We loved it! This movie is great for the whole family.

Klaus (2019)

This wonderful, traditionally animated story reimagines the origins of Santa Claus. Set in nineteenth-century Norway, it features Jesper Johns (voiced by Jason Schwartzman), an underperforming postal employee who is reassigned to the far North, where he befriends Klaus (voiced by J. K. Simmons).

Fun Facts:

- The film received an Academy Award nomination for Best Animated Feature and was the first animated film released by a streaming service to be nominated.
- As of this writing, the movie earned an approval rating of 95 percent on Rotten Tomatoes.

Movies Set at Christmastime That Aren't Necessarily About Christmas

Meet Me in St. Louis (1944)

This Judy Garland musical introduced us to the classic song "Have Yourself a Merry Little Christmas." Within the storyline of the family moving from their established St. Louis home to New York when the family patriarch gets a promotion, this song is as bittersweet as Judy Garland's dress is gorgeous. Margaret O'Brien, a popular child actress of the time, played the youngest daughter, Tootie, whose character was a delight. As a huge Judy Garland fan, I've seen this film practically a million times, and I always thrill to hear her sing "The Trolley Song."

Fun Facts:

- During filming, Judy Garland and director Vincente Minnelli fell in love and were subsequently married.

- At first, Garland hated the movie but realized Minnelli's vision: to make her look beautiful on screen. It worked.

The Bells of St. Mary's (1945)

This follow-up to the Academy Award-winning *Going My Way* (the highest-grossing film of the year) is a feel-good film starring Bing Crosby and Ingrid Bergman. Father O'Malley (Crosby) is transferred to the inner-city school St. Mary's and almost immediately falls into conflict with the headmistress, Sister Mary (Bergman). Some find the movie too schmaltzy, but this tearjerker is worth it for the aforementioned hilarious Christmas pageant scene alone.

Fun Facts:

- Director Leo McCarey was inspired to write the story in tribute to his aunt and childhood counselor, Sister Mary Benedict, one of the Sisters who helped to build the Immaculate Heart Convent in Hollywood.
- A Catholic priest served as an advisor during the shooting of the film. While the final farewell sequence was being filmed, the two lead actors decided to play a prank on the priest. Ingrid Bergman and Bing Crosby asked the director for one more take, and as "Father O'Malley" and "Sister Benedict" said goodbye, they locked lips in a passionate kiss, causing the priest advisor to jump up from his seat and roar in protest.

You've Got Mail (1998)

I love the chemistry between Tom Hanks and Meg Ryan. Plus, this movie is about books and bookstores. What's not to love?

Fun Fact:

- Nora Ephron wove in Tom Hanks's real-life affinity for collecting old typewriters into the movie but assigned this "addiction" to Greg Kinnear, who plays the part of Meg's writer boyfriend.

***Bridget Jones's Diary* (2001)**
Determined to improve herself, Bridget Jones (Renée Zellweger) chronicles her battles against her age, her weight, her job, and her pathetic love life.

Fun Facts:

- Renée Zellweger gained twenty-five pounds for the role and worked for a month at a British publishing company where she was not recognized.
- She only spoke using her English accent during the entire filming, even off-camera. At the wrap party, Hugh Grant heard her speaking "in a very strange voice," which he learned was how she really sounded.
- The original novel of the same name originated the genre called "chick lit": the single woman, battling with her mother (and sometimes, her weight), looking for love, career, and self-worth, usually in comedies. (I actually wrote a few chick-lit novels myself back in the day, including [blatant self-promotion] *Dreaming in Black & White* and *Reconstructing Natalie*.)

***The Lion, the Witch, and the Wardrobe* (1988, remade in 2005)**
This Chronicles of Narnia favorite begins when it is winter but not yet Christmas in Narnia.

***Edward Scissorhands* (1990)**
Tim Burton at his finest. Edward, played by Johnny Depp, is an unfinished humanoid who has scissors instead of hands. He's taken in by a suburban family and falls for their teenage daughter.

With a wonderful score by Danny Elfman, this "Christmas film" is delightful and bittersweet, with a lovely, touching ending.

Fun Facts:

- This was Vincent Price's last film role.
- Both Tim Burton and Danny Elfman consider this their most personal and favorite work.

While You Were Sleeping (1995)

Sandra Bullock plays hopelessly romantic Chicago Transit Authority ticket booth operator Lucy, who's mistaken for a comatose patient's fiancée at the hospital where he's recovering. Complications ensue when the man's family takes in lonely Lucy as part of their clan while he remains unconscious. This is a great romantic comedy to watch on a cold winter evening, snuggled under a quilt.

Die Hard (1988)

Hardly a "Christmas movie," but its setting at Christmas has secured it as many people's number one favorite. (We saw it when it first came out and liked the film that made Bruce Willis a star. Since so many people say it's not Christmas without watching *Die Hard*, we decided to watch it again a couple years ago to figure out why all the love? Yikes. Way too violent for us. I can't do blood and violence anymore.)

Fun Fact:

- This was Alan Rickman's first film. The English actor is beloved among Jane Austen lovers for his sensitive portrayal of Colonel Brandon in *Sense and Sensibility* and loved around the world as Snape in the Harry Potter films.) Alan had just arrived in Hollywood two days before his *Die Hard* audition and almost declined the role of Hans Gruber, fearing he'd be typecast.

Lesser-Known Gems

Mrs. Santa Claus (1996)

Angela Lansbury has never looked so lovely as in the title role of this film. Overlooked and taken for granted, Anna Claus goes for a ride in Santa's sleigh and gets stranded in New York's Lower East Side in 1910, where she becomes a part of its multicultural neighborhood. Music by Jerry Herman (*Hello, Dolly!* and *Mame*), and costarring Charles Durning, Michael Jeter, and Terrence Mann.

This is one of Michael's favorite Christmas movies. It was so hard to find on DVD that he bought a copy from Germany and had to purchase a special DVD player to watch it. While it's all in English, the back cover copy is not. "*Angela Lansbury spielt in Jerry Hermans enzückendem Musical....*"

Fun Facts:

- This was billed as the first original musical written for television since Rodgers and Hammerstein's *Cinderella* in 1957.

The Preacher's Wife (1996)

Whitney Houston plays the title role in this remake of *The Bishop's Wife*. Courtney B. Vance portrays a church pastor on the brink of burnout who prays for help—help that arrives in the form of Dudley the angel (Denzel Washington).

Fun Facts:

- This film was directed by Penny Marshall, who also directed such film favorites as *A League of Their Own* and *Big*.
- The role of Julia was written with Whitney Houston in mind.

♦ Whitney received $10 million to appear in the film; at the time, this was the highest film salary ever for a Black actress. She was also the third highest paid film actress of 1996.

Remember the Night (1940)

Barbara Stanwyck and Fred MacMurray (the dad from *My Three Sons*, the '60s TV show) star in the holiday rom-com about a shoplifter (Stanwyck) who is invited to spend Christmas with the assistant district attorney (MacMurray) and his family, rather than in jail.

Christmas in Connecticut (1945)

Another Barbara Stanwyck rom-com, this time about a newspaper food writer who can't cook but must pretend to be a housewife at Christmastime in order to fool her war hero fan.

Prancer (1989)

Michael says we saw this movie years ago when it was first released. Since we didn't meet until 1991, I'm pretty sure he saw it before we started dating. I wouldn't have forgotten this heartwarming, poignant tale of a nine-year-old girl who still believes in Santa Claus. Guaranteed to fill you with Christmas spirit. (With the bonus of Sam Elliott as the jaded, depressed widower who's lost his wife.)

The Best Christmas Pageant Ever (2024)

The delightful and poignant movie adaptation of Michael's favorite Christmas book is a new addition to our Christmas movie list. Not to be confused with the '80s Loretta Swit version, it showcases the Herdman family, "the worst kids in the history of the world," featuring features Lauren Graham (Lorelai from *The Gilmore Girls*) in a small role.

Honorable Mention

The Sound of Music (1965)

Although it isn't set at Christmastime and also doesn't even mention any winter holidays, this beloved musical was broadcast on TV every year on Christmas evening when I was growing up. Many people associate it with the season. As a matter of fact, one year, Michael was writing an article for his company newsletter and polled dozens of his coworkers about their favorite Christmas movie ever. Along with the usual suspects, *The Sound of Music* got several votes.

Clearly, I'm not the only one who considers it one of my favorite things.

> "The best way to spread Christmas cheer is singing loud for all to hear." —Will Ferrell in *Elf*

Note: Obviously, tastes are subjective, and there are many holiday movies missing from this list. I've included movies we like and ones that frequently make the top Christmas movie lists. As well, you'll notice there are no Hallmark Christmas movies on this list. Nothing personal; we don't subscribe to the Hallmark Channel, so we have never watched any.

I hope this list prompts you to try some Christmas movies you've never seen before. Next year, I plan to check out the Finnish film *Rare Exports*, recommended so highly by our friends Ryan and Ella.

See you at the movies!

Love came down at Christmas,
Love all lovely, love divine;
Love was born at Christmas;
Star and angels gave the sign.
—Christina Rossetti

About the Author

Laura J. Walker is a bestselling, award-winning author of more than twenty books, including *Thanks for the Mammogram!*, *Mentalpause and Other Midlife Laughs*, and *Reconstructing Natalie* (Women of Faith Novel of the Year). She has been nominated for an Agatha Award and a Lefty Award for her mystery novels, and she won the American Christian Fiction Writers Best Novel award for her fiction debut, *Dreaming in Black and White*. An air force veteran formerly stationed in England, Laura is an avid Anglophile who lives in Northern California with her Renaissance man of a husband, Michael ("Mr. Christmas"), and their two rescue "terror-iers" in a wannabe English cottage where they watch British mysteries and dream of England. They attend their neighborhood Episcopal church, where they used to sing in the choir until their voices went south.